We Are One:
A Challenge to Traditional Christianity

By Ellwood Norquist

Cosmic Connection Publishing
250 N. Arcadia Avenue #904
Tucson, Arizona 85711

Cover painting by
Michael D. Booth

ISBN 0-9646995-2-4

Cosmic Connection Publishing
250 N. Arcadia Avenue #904
Tucson, Arizona 85711

Printed by

**MISSION
POSSIBLE**
Commercial
Printing

P.O. Box 1526 • Sedona, Arizona 86339

Dedication

To the loving memory of Danny.

About the Cover

I imagine that many readers, looking at the cover of this book for the first time, may pause to wonder what connection, if any, it has to the contents of the book.

I hope that my short explanation helps the reader to find in the illustration a small feeling of what I believe Mr. Norquist's book is pointing out to us in far more detail.

The outermost swirling gold conveys to me the feeling of the pure energy of the universe, the feeling of the One out of which all is made, but which can never really be depicted. It is gold because the ancients used the color as a symbol for the metal. Gold is precious, beautiful, malleable, earnestly sought after and must be purified by fire.

The swirling gold frames the Mandelbrot fractal "window," which is a mathematical representation of the way in which the world of matter is constructed, and displays the infinite harmonies from which everything in our world emerges, whether it be animal, vegetable or mineral. Each tiny, lacelike indentation contains the form of the whole ad infinitum. These algorithms are used by all growing things, whether they be crystalline or living matter. Within this window is the sensible universe of energy-matter.

At the lower center is Leonardo's depiction of our physical vehicle for experiencing this miracle of life. It too is made of gold — spiritual gold. This reflects the light of the pure Logos, depicted in the upper section, which bathes and illuminates all.

Michael D. Booth
Cover Artist

Acknowledgments

The thoughts and ideas expressed in this collection of essays result from years of reading and study, of experiencing life in diverse areas of the world and in work environments where I was involved with peoples of many races and cultural backgrounds. And for my life and history I owe a lot to my parents, teachers and others who taught me intellectual curiosity and a yearning for peace with my fellows and with my Creator.

I am grateful to friends who believed in me and my writing — especially to Eric Juren, a published writer — who in numerous telephone conversations and personal meetings encouraged me to persevere with my manuscript. Thanks also to Jeannie Boone, Ed and Gerry Birney, Rex Pickering, Kerry Hoffman, Rev. Warren Chester and Drs. Frederick and Rita Rogers.

A special thanks to my son Eddie Gonzalez, who was always there with his loving support and his faith in me.

Big thanks and appreciation to Michael Booth, my New York City friend from years past, who produced the beautiful and meaningful cover for this work.

In the final stages of preparing the manuscript for publication I owe great thanks to Margaret Pinyan, who edited the work. She, having come out of Christian Fundamentalism like myself, understood well what I was trying to communicate and was very helpful in suggesting an addition here or a deletion there of an idea or phrase, besides eliminating my numerous errors of punctuation.

Last but not least, thanks to the city of Tucson, which gave me, after living in a big, bustling city for years, time and space to be quiet, to think, to meditate and to enjoy the beauty of the desert, the majesty of the mountains and even the wildlife in my own backyard.

Preface

I awoke one morning from a very vivid dream. I roused myself gently and in the semi-darkness (the sun was just about to emerge from its place of nightly hiding and break forth over the eastern Rincon Mountains in its usual brilliant morning display) I groped for my pad and pencil and quickly wrote what I still clearly saw nearly word for word, a message from my dreaming state. After nearly filling an entire page, I stumbled back into bed and promptly fell asleep.

After rising the second time an hour or so later, I half remembered (or was that part of the dream? I wondered) getting out of bed and writing something on my desk pad. Yes, there it was, a page of material in my handwriting. Reading it, I said to myself, That sounds like the beginning of a book. Up to that moment I had not thought about writing a book, but within four months I had completed a manuscript I entitled *With Love, A Letter to My Christian Fundamentalist Friends.*

The manuscript was enthusiastically accepted by the first publisher to whom I submitted it but who ultimately dropped it because of financial and other problems. I put the manuscript aside, and although my inaction seems strange to me now, I did little more to get it into print. Meanwhile more than one psychic told me that the manuscript would be published, but only after I had written and published a second book. This collection of essays, my second work, came after a hiatus of about three years.

It seems to me now, after those three years, that I was delayed in writing the thoughts and concepts appearing in this small volume, for most of them did not originate until the climate of opinion was better prepared for accepting them. I believe that we have reached a time in history when people are beginning to take charge of their own destiny, no longer leaving it to elected officials or other authorities to regulate their lives and no longer blindly accepting every truth that their religious leaders propound. We have reached a time in history, it seems to me, when humanity for the first time is ready and able to come to grips with his problems on a more enlightened level.

We have had great illumined souls in the past. They have appeared in all cultures and in all parts of the world, but their illumination and teachings affected only the few among their immediate followers. The teaching of Buddha was heard only by those he personally touched; the fervor of Savonarola affected only the Florentines; the saintliness of St. Francis was not known beyond the hills of Tuscany and the halls of the Vatican. Jesus, in the immediate period of his life, was known only to a small group in a remote corner of the Roman Empire.

Today seems different. Today the illumined insights of Buddha, a Lao Tsu, a Confucius, could be instantly communicated to all corners of the globe. We live in an information age. We might see Buddha testifying before the United Nations, Mohammed on the evening news and Jesus being questioned by Larry King.

Each age has seen and understood the human condition from a new and broader perspective than the one that preceded it, and in our time the information age is encouraging as never before the people of the world to face not only the problems of the world, but themselves. The world has become a global village. We are beginning to realize that indeed we are all one. We are one in our humanity, one in spirit and one with God. We will continue to focus on and work to change man's inhumanity to man until we learn to love our neighbor, to accept one another as we are, to shift our focus from our superficial differences to our human commonalities. We will continue to grapple with these problems until we decide to leave our violent nature behind, to think, live and breathe peace. As a lady friend of mine who leads a discussion group I often attend says, "We have to stop hating and start loving." I think she is right!

I believe that we are within reach of the goal of creating a planet of peace, prosperity and love. With the help of the angelic forces that are now bombarding our earth with vibrations of love, the "millennium" is fast approaching. To many, the opposite may seem more obvious. Certainly, one must recognize that at one level of understanding we can say that the world has never been more violent than at present and that corruption in government and business has never been more prevalent. The forces of negativity and separation are at work as never before. True! But I believe that these forces will soon lose out. They are fighting a desperate, last-ditch effort against the rising tide of the vibrations of love and acceptance. This rising tide of goodness, of God, of love, will win. The time of winnowing is upon us. The time for the wheat to be separated from the chaff is now!

I feel uniquely qualified to write this challenge to traditional Christianity. I was brought up in a fundamentalist Christian home in a small community in Minnesota. Our life was centered around the Baptist church where I, together with my older brother and my parents, attended Sunday school and two church services each Sunday and a prayer meeting each Thursday evening. At the age of fourteen I was baptized in Fish Lake by our pastor, a student at Bethel Seminary in St. Paul. For many years I faithfully read the scriptures, attended church services and diligently worked to bring my "unsaved" friends to Jesus. At the time, perhaps, this was well and good. But after years of study and contemplation, I now see my relationship to my Creator in a much more satisfying and fulfilling way. I feel that the average Christian limits his God to simply being a superhuman. He sees his Creator as an entity in the image of man and attributes to Him human characteristics. And the average Christian also limits himself, seeing himself as a sinner in danger of eternal separation from his Creator.

The essays in this short work are on many diverse subjects, but they have one common thread of what I consider to be a fundamental truth: that we are one with each other and one with God.

When reading the essays, it is suggested that the first four or five be read in the order in which they appear. The reader then can peruse the remaining essays in any order. In the reading of any one essay you may have questions that do not seem to be answered there but that may be found in another essay.

To the reader who is exposed for the first time to what might be termed New Age thought, I ask only that you keep an open mind and thoughtfully and prayerfully consider the spiritual (as opposed to religious) concepts here presented.

One final word. Throughout my writing of this work I have used the traditional masculine forms when referring to God. No sexism is intended, but to use such phrases as "His/Her," "He/She," or "Mother/Father God" over and over would, I feel, be clumsy and interfere with the smooth flow of the work. As we all understand, God is neither masculine nor feminine, nor is God *both* masculine and feminine. God is simply *being.*

Contents

Introduction   ix
1 ✦ The Nature of God: Duality vs. Nonduality   1
2 ✦ The Nature of Reality: A Scientific View   5
3 ✦ The Nature of Reality: A Spiritual View   13
4 ✦ In the Beginning   19
5 ✦ Good vs. Evil   25
6 ✦ The Separation   31
7 ✦ The Cosmic Christ   39
8 ✦ Sin and Salvation   43
9 ✦ The Wages of Sin   53
10 ✦ The Fear of the Lord   59
11 ✦ God's Blessing   63
12 ✦ The Love of God   65
13 ✦ The Will of God   67
14 ✦ Sexuality   69
15 ✦ "I Am the Light of the World"   77
16 ✦ The Word of God   79
17 ✦ Jesus   83
18 ✦ A Story of a Past Life   87
19 ✦ On Reincarnation   91
20 ✦ The God of the Old Testament   107
21 ✦ Judgment   113
22 ✦ Forgiveness   121
23 ✦ The Second Coming   129
24 ✦ A.D. 2011   133
25 ✦ Today   139
A Fundamentalist Questions a New Ager   143
Reading List   151

Introduction

In those formative and retrievable years that begin at age three and start to fade at about age seven, my closest friend was an elder of the kingdom of nature: a majestic old Elm Tree located on the Minnesota side of Lake Pepin, just south of Red Wing. It was one of the patriarchal presences that added a sense of wisdom to Frontenac, a beautiful but decaying village first settled by George Gerrard, a general of the Union Army during the Civil War.

This is neither a book about Gerrard nor about trees. It is, however, a book about wisdom. And it was that patriarch Elm that gave me my first lessons in wisdom and provided an invitation to reach beyond the traditional Christianity of the churches. You will please note that Elm Tree is in upper case. The reason may not be obvious to the reader, but the Elm Tree was my first experience of the word becoming flesh. In those years, which unfortunately do not last forever, that Elm Tree was God incarnate to Me (note: "Me" is also in upper case). Elm Tree taught me that what I saw with my eyes and heard with my ears was not as important as what I saw with the "eyes of my eyes" and heard with the "ears of my ears." Elm Tree spoke to those subtle eyes and taught me to see with those subtle ears. Elm Tree made it clear that often what people said was not what they meant, and that words, rules and facts could often become the enemy of truth.

But I was taught a greater and more lasting truth at the feet of this majestic Elm. Through our communion I came to learn that what was of ultimate importance to me and to my own growth was not what was written *in* the lines, but rather what was written *between* the lines. By this my Elm Tree was suggesting, in its parasensory form of communication, that there are no prefixed, concrete, definitely objectifiable meanings or definitions. There are instead limitless possibilities that can be discovered, depending upon my mind's (and heart's) capacity to reach beyond appearances into the limitless void of spirit. Elm Tree did not speak these words literally. The words, rather, became flesh in my experience. More accurately, the words of Elm Tree became incarnate in the consciousness of my cells, not to be born in concrete expression or printed words until this much later time, as you read the likes of this book you hold before you.

This is a book that will suggest to the reader the possibilities for new ideas to shape themselves from old and well-defined images and orthodoxies. The title itself challenges us to take a new look at traditional Christianity. It even suggests that Christianity, with its strong, literal emphasis on "oneness" (John 17:21-22), may actually have caused more separation than reconciliation. This book addresses that disparity.

It suggests to the reader that there might be a more fulfilling way to deal with Christianity than by perceiving humankind as foundationally sinful, separate and in dire need of salvation. Ellwood Norquist draws from a variety of disciplines and resources to point the reader in a direction that will assist in defining humankind as foundationally divine, in union with its Creator, and already saved, with the simple suggestion that all we need do is "wake up" (much like Alice did in Wonderland) to the notion that we really never did leave the Garden. To assist in this process Mr. Norquist draws from *A Course in Miracles,* the field of quantum physics, the Gnostic traditions, the transmissions of Bartholomew and Edgar Cayce, the mystery traditions of the ancient past, the writings of Matthew Fox and Elaine Pagels, and from his own experience.

The book is based on the premise that God never drove us out of the Garden. Rather, a "deep sleep" fell upon us, and even now we are in the process of awakening to our own divine inheritance. This book takes concepts that have been complicated by many recent authors, places those concepts within the experience of the author, and conveys meanings that are both simple and practical for the pilgrim aspiring toward spiritual awakening and renewal.

The book flies in the face of many Christian orthodoxies. It is not an academic treatise but tends toward an experiential confession and affirmation. The author leads the reader through varieties of religious orthodoxies (original sin, separation from God, salvation, the fear of God, judgment and death) and ends up where we have always longed to be. Just like the Prodigal Son, we are welcomed home by a parent who never anticipated that we would leave. The truth is, as Ellwood points out so clearly and simply, we never did leave.

The weakest chapter in the book, in my opinion, deals with "The God of the Old Testament." I feel Mr. Norquist was overly zealous in proof-texting the Hebrew writings to convey a God of wrath, fury, jealousy and fear, a God without mercy Who condoned slavery and adultery, and Who demeaned women. What he missed of the Hebrew writings was its major focus of mercy and compassion . . . the God Who constantly received back His exiled and wandering people, Who repeatedly supplied them with the very things they needed for their own liberation, and Who commissioned them/us to "do justice, love mercy, and walk humbly."

Christian Fundamentalists will not like this book. They will not likely place it in their bookstores, nor will they agree with many of its premises. A growing number of Christians today are not only unwilling to read between the lines, they are also resistant to anything other than literal interpretations. This book does not represent such an approach. In fact, it radically challenges the premise that Christians are unique, special or even "chosen," and substitutes for those beliefs the notion that all (male, female, Christian, Jew, Muslim, Buddhist, Hindu, Pagan, heterosexual, homosexual, rich, poor) are embraced, accepted and received by the love of a God Who knows no separation or duality, only oneness. The wise old Elm Tree of my childhood would have appreciated this book. I hope you do too.

Dr. P. David Wilkinson

P. David Wilkinson, Rel. D., is pastor of St. Francis in the Foothills United Methodist Church in Tucson, Arizona, a United Methodist congregation that includes Christian, Jews, Muslims, heterosexuals, homosexuals and those who reach beyond orthodoxies into "yet larger rooms" of spiritual encounter with God.

the presence of evil in our world? If only God and light existed from the beginning, how is it possible that a separation from God could have happened? How was it possible that darkness emerged out of the pure light and love of the Creator?

We are then faced, it seems to me, with quite a dilemma. How or why did humanity, God's creation, fall? How did sin enter our world? How can mankind find its way back to be reunited with his Creator? Christian theology does not have any clear explanation for how the devil or evil emerged from the light. It teaches that evil and the devil are outside of God, not being part of His nature. In a sense, however, this almost suggests the dualistic nature of God, indicating that evil must have existed from the very beginning.

Would the reader be willing to consider that there may be a more honest, more realistic, more scriptural answer to the dilemma of evil vs. goodness, of sin and its consequences? Would the reader be willing to consider that there may be a much more satisfying way, a happier way, of dealing with the problem of the Fall, the separation from God? I believe there is such a way —a much better way.

In the essays that follow we will develop the concept that humankind, being the perfect and eternal creation of a perfect and eternal Creator, was never separated from his Creator and therefore doesn't need to be saved from evil or sin in the usual sense of Christianity's teachings, especially the teachings of fundamentalist Christianity. Moreover, this happy idea is not in any way contrary to the holy scriptures. It is, I believe, in strict accord with the scriptures.

If the reader, then, is ready with a loving heart and an open mind, we will proceed in our search for some possible answers to the various questions we have formulated.

✧ 2

The Nature of Reality: A Scientific View

Sit down before fact like a little child, and be prepared to give
up every preconceived notion, follow humbly wherever and to
whatever abysses Nature leads, or you shall learn nothing.

— T. H. Huxley

What is reality? What is this marvelous creation of God that we as humans are a part of? Those are the questions that our physicists are grappling with in these last years of our twentieth century.

Science is in the midst of an almost incredible paradigm shift. Our scientists, especially the physicists, are proclaiming major changes in the way they attempt to answer the question, What *is* reality? Yes, as a result of new scientific findings and attitudes we are undergoing a major change in our cosmology — a major shift in the way we see ourselves in the cosmos.

Every society, every culture of the world, has always had a cosmology, a way of explaining to its people their place and purpose within the universe. It is how its people perceived reality, the pattern that made sense to them and that they felt comfortable with. Today we have our modern cosmology, far different from the cosmologies of the ancient world that we study, but we need, as much as ever, a pattern, a road map of sorts, and a logical explanation of who we are and how we fit in with the workings of the cosmos.

Our personal cosmology, the way we see ourselves in the cosmos, is largely determined by two things: what the scientists tell us and what the theologians tell us. For most of us, I suspect that our personal cosmology is determined by a varying mixture of the two. Those with strong religious backgrounds tilt to religious explanations, whereas others may lean to scientific views. The ongoing debate of evolution vs. creation is a good example of how sometimes the teachings of science do not agree with the teachings of the theologians. In any debate of science vs. religion we might keep in mind the words of P. D. Ouspensky, a philosopher of the early twentieth century, "A religion contradicting science and a science contradicting religion are equally false."[1]

Man's way of relating himself to the universe has undergone a number of paradigm shifts throughout our history. The most recent major shift in man's thinking occurred in the late medieval and early Renaissance times. The prevailing world view up to that time had been that the world is flat, the earth is the center of the universe and the sun and the stars and planets revolve around the earth. This adequately explained the way things seemed to the medieval man — it made him comfortable with his place in the universe.

Then along came Copernicus, Kepler, Galileo and, a bit later, Newton. Everything changed, but not immediately. The religious views of the Catholic Church prevailed for a time, not allowing the new knowledge to be taught. Only slowly did the Church come to an accommodation with the new scientific findings.

A whole new cosmology was born. Our sun became the center of our local system, our planet was round, like all celestial bodies, and it revolved around our sun. Man began to see himself in his relation to all of God's creation in a different light. The great paradigm shift had changed in very fundamental ways our religious beliefs, our scientific understanding and our philosophical view of life in general.

Now we seem to be on the edge of another paradigm shift, and again many scientists are leading the way and conservative theologians of the leading religions are dragging their feet. This new shift in our understanding is an even more dramatic change from present thinking than was the shift in the Middle Ages to the people of that era. And it is equally disrupting, if not more so, to the closed minds of the present as the new views of the earlier period were to that earlier generation.

This change in scientific thinking is principally a result of two major developments: quantum physics, which built upon and, one might even say, replaced classical physics; and the development and understanding of the hologram.

The two main principles of classical physics – the physics that I learned in my college days and, I suspect, that my readers learned (excepting the present generation of students) – are that the universe is objective and that it is predictable.

Classical physics, from Newton to Einstein, saw our world and the universe made up of particles of matter. Earlier, the atom was the smallest known particle of matter; then smaller and smaller particles were discovered and more and more brilliant mathematical formulas devised, all of which increased greatly our knowledge of our world and our universe. Thus for the classical physicist, the universe is objective: There is a world "out there."

The world and the cosmos being objective, made up of physical matter, demonstrated that the universe was determinable – that is, ultimately predictable. So to the classical physicist, when man finally learned all the facts and mathematical formulas that governed matter, reliable predictions could be made concerning how matter would behave. Much of the future could then be predicted.

Today, however, there is a new physics, quantum physics, which goes far beyond the limited truths and understanding of classical physics. The classical physicist asked the question, "How, after the Big Bang and the beginning of time, did consciousness gradually evolve from physical matter?" The question has not been answered, and now physicists have come to the conclusion that it is the wrong question and therefore can never be answered. Now quantum physics is asking the question, "How did consciousness create matter?"

Contradicting the classical physicist, the quantum physicist claims that mind, not matter, is primary (consciousness came first) and demonstrates the indeterminacy of the particle (there really is no "real world" out there). The increasingly small particles are seen to act as both particles and waves, and thus are not particles at all. The bottom line seems to be, simply stated, that *matter is materialized consciousness.* The cosmos is not just one big machine any longer; it is one big thought!

Those startling conclusions are largely the result of two men, working independently at first, who experienced new breakthroughs in thought that brought mankind to the new paradigm shift. David Bohm was an American physicist who did his work at the University of London. Karl Pribram was a neurophysiologist at Stanford University. Their new views of the cosmos are based on the breakthrough ideas of quantum physics as discussed above and on the development of holographic lensless photography.

A hologram is produced by a laser split into two separate beams, one bounced off an object, the other directed at the light reflected from the object by the first beam. The resulting interference pattern appears on the plate and is similar to the patterns produced when pebbles are tossed into a pond.

The image that is projected does not appear on the plate. However, when an identical laser is passed through the plate, the original object is seen in its complete three-dimensional form. One can walk around and even through the projection. The entire three-dimensional image is an illusion; it doesn't really exist physically at all.

The most startling thing about the hologram, however, is that if an identical laser is projected through the smallest portion of the holographic plate, *the entire image* appears once again! For example, if the image is one of a collie dog and the plate is broken into pieces, the image of the entire collie could be projected from each fragment. Any part of the hologram reproduces the entire hologram. Each and every part of the holographic plate contains the entire image. Each part is the whole!

Carl Jung, years earlier and without any knowledge of the holographic model, claimed that our dreams, our myths and even our religious visions come from the same unconscious source, the unconscious mind shared by all. He was saying much the same as today's physicists. *Each part is the whole.*

Pribram used the startling developments in holography to show that the human brain is itself a hologram. Each small part of the brain contains all memory, because the brain is not locally selective in its memory, as formerly believed. The human brain stores 280,000,000,000,000,000,000 bits of information; a holographic plate about the size of a postage stamp can store over 50,000 pages of written material.

It's important to note that a holographic image is a virtual image. That is, it takes up no space, although it appears to be in space — just as one's image in a mirror seems to be in space but is not; it is merely a reflection, an illusion.

While Karl Pribram was working with the brain as a hologram, David Bohm was working on the quantum theory of physics and was coming to similar conclusions about the illusory nature of matter. For some time, physicists had been confused by the behavior of electrons, those small bits of "matter" that behave as both a wave and a particle. It was also upsetting that one single electron could pass through two holes at the same time. They found that electrons and even smaller bits of so-called matter have no dimensions at all. They do not seem even to exist. And these small bits of matter bombarded against each other create interference patterns like that of the hologram. Bohm showed that location doesn't exist, either. One could not say that one bit of matter was separate from another bit of matter. Any point in space is the same as another point in space. Extending Einstein's idea that space and time are not separate from each other but are parts of a space-time continuum, Bohm showed that not only space and time, but everything, is part of the continuum. Taking the work of Bohm and Pribram together has given us a profound new way of seeing ourselves in the cosmos. It has given us a new cosmology fundamentally different from our previous understanding. Michael Talbot sums up their work this way: "Our brains mathematically construct objective reality by interpreting frequencies that are ultimately projections from another dimension, a deeper order of existence that is beyond both space and time: The brain is a hologram enfolded in a holographic universe."[2]

In other words, the conclusion based on the holographic model is that the physical universe really does not exist as previously understood. Each bit of matter contains the whole. Indeed, each bit is the whole. We are not looking at a holographic universe; we are part of the hologram and *we do not exist as physical beings at all.* As St. Francis said long ago, "What we are looking for is what is looking."

In summary, we see that we are indeed experiencing a major shift in our cosmology, our way of understanding ourselves and our universe. Quantum physicists and other leading-edge scientists now portray a human being as much more than a physical machine. We and everything else in our so-called physical surroundings are a part of the consciousness that existed outside space and time before the beginning. We are indeed part of the Light that created All That Is.

In our next essay we come to the same conclusions. Science and spirit no longer are at odds. Science and spirit are bridged. They are one; we all are one!

---

[1]P. D. Ouspensky, quoted in *Bridging Science and Spirit* by Norman Friedman. Living Lake Books, St. Louis, Missouri, 1994, p. 19.

[2]Michael Talbot, *The Holographic Universe.* Harper Collins Publishers, New York, 1991, p. 54.

✧ 3

The Nature of Reality: A Spiritual View

Outside of God there is nothing but nothing.
Who is God? What is God?
I reply: Isness. Isness is God.
What is God? God is.

— Meister Eckhart (1260-1329)

"I Am" was God's response to Abraham when asked who
He was. "God is." Saying anything further is limiting. When
we make such statements as "God is good, God is merciful, God
is compassionate," are we not limiting Him? When we say, "God
is just," are we not suggesting the possibility of God being unjust?
Can we truthfully say anything about God without limiting Him
in some way, unless we say, "God is"?

Meister Eckhart, a great churchman of the Middle Ages
quoted above, understood that truth when he proclaimed, "Outside of God there is nothing but nothing." Everything created
by God is a part of God. Outside of God's creation there is nothing! All of God's creation is an extension of His very essence,

13

His being, His love. The creation is an extended part of the Creator. There is no dividing line, no separation. The Creator and the created are one. God created everything in His image; that is, as an extension of His spirit, His essence. What God created, therefore, is part of the very spirit of God, is part of the very essence of God and is, therefore, as perfect and as eternal as He is. There are no spatial or temporal qualities to His creation. The creation is as God is.

Human beings, on the other hand, create or make not by extension of their being but by projecting their thoughts, their ideas, into the world of space and time. God's creation shares the qualities of the Creator, the qualities of being perfect and eternal. Likewise, whatever mankind makes shares the qualities of its maker. What mankind makes is temporal and spatial. Our physical life and everything we make is limited in time and space.

In graduate school at Columbia in New York City, I was pleasantly surprised when one of my professors said that a teacher, when teaching history or in fact any discipline, should be attempting to answer only one question: "Who am I?" When I later began teaching ancient history to high school students at a prestigious private prep school in Riverdale, New York, I recalled that comment and often would get into philosophical discussions dealing with that question. After asking my students, "Who are you?" and getting the usual answers such as "I am John Doe," "I am a human being," "I am a physical body with such and such attributes" etc., I would then, in attempting to get the students to see the point I was trying to make, follow with the questions, "Do you have a body? Do you have a mind? Do you have a soul?"

After they typically answered yes to the questions, I would then ask, "If you *have* a body, if you *have* a mind, if you *have* a soul, then who or what are *you?* If you *have* these things, then you must be something different from what you have." Together, then, my students and I would conclude that man does not *have* a soul; instead, man *is* a soul, a soul residing temporarily in a body.

I believe that God created the soul of man, the real you, the real me. God created man in His own image, in His own essence, as an extension of His eternal love. The soul, our real being, perfect and eternal, is temporarily residing in a physical body not of God's creation. If the body were God's creation, it would be perfect and eternal. Our bodies, made by the outward projection of man's mind, live in time and space and then die. What God creates (the soul) is eternal. What man makes (the body) is temporal. I think this helps to make more clear and understandable the oft-quoted verse 23 of Romans 6: "The wages of sin is death [of the body], but the gift of God is eternal life."

But how do we account for evil in our world? How did man become separated from his Creator? If we are one with Him, a very part of His being, how is it possible to be apart from Him?

We have, since the Fall, been living with the fear and the guilt of being separate from God. But in actuality, I believe, the separation from God never happened! God did not draw a dividing line between Himself and His creation. Man did! Could God separate a part of Himself from Himself? Man in his guilt imagined that God threw him out of the Garden of Eden, as recorded in the mythical story from the book of Genesis in our Holy Bible.

Let us keep in mind that what man makes is imperfect and

temporal and what God creates is perfect and eternal. As the Bible has indicated, this world, the stars, the planets and all elements of the starry firmament will one day disappear. The structures of mankind will no longer be needed. Only what was created by God will remain. Even our physical body is not real in a spiritual sense. Our physical body dies; our soul lives on eternally. Our soul was created by God. Our body was made to protect the diminishing light of the soul, and the cosmos was made as a place in which to hide from the Creator.

The world you see is an illusion of a world. God did not create it, for what He creates must be as eternal as Himself. Yet there is nothing in the world you see that will endure forever. Some things will last in time a little while longer than others. But the time will come when all things visible will have an end."[1]

"God will wipe away our tears." We will forget everything that happened in our earthly lives. How is that possible, we may ask. I believe it's because in God's reality our earthly physical lives never happened. In God's reality all our earthly experiences are an illusion, a dream lived out in time to obtain experience and growth on our journey back to an awareness of who we are, a part of that great ocean of love, God, from whom we were never separated.

We are hiding in our created world from God, yes, but since we are an extension of God, a part of the Creator, we are really hiding from our true self. We are a son of God, but we are ignorant of that truth. We believe that we are separate from our Creator, lost in time and space and in need of someone or something to heal the separation.

16

In bridging science and spirit, it is clearly seen, I believe, that the spiritual concept that we are one with God and that each one of us is one drop in an ocean of love, closely parallels the physicist's view of the oneness of all creation. Quantum physics shows that All-That-Is is consciousness, or light, outside of space and time and that our three-dimensional physical manifestation in space and time has been an unfoldment of that consciousness. Science does not name the eternal consciousness that existed before time: the spiritual/religious community does. It calls it God. Science and spirit are ONE!

---

[1]*A Course In Miracles, Manual for Teachers.* Foundation for Inner Peace, Huntington Station, New York, 1975, p. 81.

ory of relativity, demolished the idea of absolute time. Time and space, according to many of our scientists, depend on where you are in space and how fast you are moving.

Since time began with the Big Bang, according to the creation theory of the same name, space has been continuously expanding. The formerly held concept that space was in a steady state of existence has been abandoned by Stephen W. Hawking and other leading-edge scientists. They say that both space and time are in flux, moving relative to each other. Time had a beginning, and space and everything in it had a beginning. What had a beginning must have an ending. "Time shall be no more," the scriptures proclaim.

Assuming the above, then, we can say that time began with the Big Bang and that time will end after the universe's complete cycle of expansion and contraction. A way of picturing this concept is to imagine yourself in the center of an inflated balloon that gradually increases in size around you. Then one day the inflation comes to a halt, and after a moment of rest the air gradually begins to be withdrawn. Far East religions call this cosmic process of expansion and contraction the inbreath and outbreath of God (see "A.D. 2011").

Keep in mind that what God creates is infinite and eternal, as infinite and eternal as God Himself, and that time and space and everything in it is finite[1] and temporal and therefore only an illusion, to pass away when we no longer need it for our experience. *A Course in Miracles* says it this way:

> The world you see is an illusion of a world. God did not create it, for what He creates must be eternal as Himself.

> Yet there is nothing in the world you see that will endure forever. Some things will last in time a little while longer than others. But the time will come when all things visible will have an end.[2]

The Bible says much the same: "And God shall wipe away all tears from their eyes; and there shall be no more death . . . for the former things are passed away."[3]

Going back to the "beginning": "In the beginning the gods created the heavens and the earth." Yes, gods (plural!) is correct. The original Hebrew of Genesis does indeed use the plural form of the word for God. Translators decided to make it a singular God to conform to their misunderstanding.

It seems, then, that God, the First Cause, the Unmoved Mover, is our single source of all that exists. This Prime Mover God created the "morning and the night," the Gold and Silver Rays, and all the angels, archangels, cherubim, seraphim and the elohim — the hierarchies of beings. These are the gods that created the physical world and the starry firmament above that so capture our imaginations and stir our unconscious memories. The Gold and Silver Rays were given the task of the making of the worlds — our planet and all of the universes in the entire cosmos. This has been accomplished over trillions of years, as man counts time, and will remain in our illusion for as long as it takes us to become fully aware of our divinity and realize that we are God's only begotten son and daughters in whom He is well pleased.

The self or ego uses this world to perpetuate the illusion of sin, fear and guilt in an attempt to make the separation from God real, but the Holy Spirit, that part of the trinity that speaks to us and bridges the supposed gap between us and God, shows us that this world is our classroom, our place to experience, our place to learn the lesson of love and acceptance. When that lesson is learned, it seems to me, the illusion of the world and everything in it will be no more because in God's reality it never existed.

---

[1]Some may argue that space is infinite. Stephen Hawking, however, says, "When one combines general relativity with the uncertainty principle of quantum mechanics, it is possible for both space and time to be finite without any edges or boundaries." *A Brief History of Time,* New York, Bantam Books, 1988, p. 44.

[2]*A Course in Miracles, Manual For Teachers,* p. 81.

[3]Revelation 21:4.

Good vs. Evil

What seem to be evils are not actually such.

— Seneca (B.C. 4 A.D. 66)

Over two thousand years ago Socrates said that if one knows the good, he will do the good. Do you agree with Socrates?

Would the alcoholic who ends up homeless and friendless after losing his job, his family, his money and even his self-esteem have taken his first drink if he knew what would be the end result? According to Socrates, that future alcoholic would not have taken that first drink. But did the future alcoholic *really* know to what degradation he would fall? He might have been warned by family, friends and others but thought that he was different; that he understood the possible consequences but had sufficient self-control, strength of character; that he would know when to stop. But had he known absolutely that that first drink would be his undoing, he would have declared no to any and all temptations to imbibe that first time. That is what Socrates was saying.

What about you and me? Would we do only God's will if we really knew that only by following His will would we be peaceful, successful and wonderfully joyful? Why do we so easily succumb to temptations, do what we believe to be wrong, do what we know is harmful to ourselves and to others? Why are we so easily persuaded to wrong actions and thoughts? Why do we listen to the ego instead of the Holy Spirit's promptings from within?

Epictetus, one of the Stoic writers of the early Roman Empire, put it this way: "When a man speaks evil or does evil to you, remember that he does or says it because he thinks it is fitting for him. It is not possible for him to follow what seems good to you, but only what seems good to him . . ." In other words, a human does what he believes is good, though others may consider it evil. Each of us, according to Epictetus, is doing the best we know how to do.

Perhaps there is no such thing as evil! Consider for a moment that evil may not really exist. Can evil exist within God's reality? If God is pure love, where is the possibility of evil? If everything that is real was created as an extension of God, then everything that is real is good, perfect and eternal. The extended creation of a perfect and eternal God must be as perfect and eternal as the Creator. Could it be otherwise?

Everything in our physical world is based on polarities: up-down, good-bad, beautiful-ugly etc. For example, if everything were beautiful, would we have the concept for ugly? Would we even have the concept for beautiful? If there were no such thing as war or warlike thoughts, we would not have the concepts of war and peace, or even the words "war" or "peace."

Consider the polarity of cold vs. heat. The sun is the source of all heat in our solar system. What is the source of cold? Ice? The polar regions? No, there doesn't seem to be a source of coldness. It seems that there is no such thing as cold, coldness being merely the absence of heat.

The polarity of light vs. darkness is perhaps an even better illustration. The sun is the source of all light within our solar system. There is no source of darkness, darkness being simply the absence of light. A flashlight can dispel the darkness, but there is no such thing as a flashdark that can dispel the light!

Likewise, evil vs. good: I believe that God is the source of all goodness, for He is pure love. Evil is the absence of good, there being no source for evil, if God alone was in the beginning. (See Chapter 1 for a more thorough discussion of the nature of God, examining duality vs. nonduality.)

It seems to me that the apparent existence of evil on earth is part of the illusion of living inside time and space. In God's reality, where there are no spatial or temporal qualities, there is only pure love. Where there is only pure love, its polarity, evil, seems to be only an illusion.

After all I have said about evil being only an illusion, there may be a deeper reality that better explains the concept of evil. According to the new physics of David Bohm and others (see the earlier essay, "The Nature of Reality: A Scientific View"), all polarities or opposites are not really opposites at all. What we see as negativities and opposites really represent deep unities that man cannot truly comprehend. In this sense, evil and goodness are necessary parts of a whole, neither of which is better than the other. Eastern philosophical thought helps us here, as it teaches the same concept, that truth is grasped through the synthesis of apparent opposites and that humanity's distorted perceptions cause incorrect assumptions. Seth says the same thing: "Opposites have validity only in your own system of reality. They are a part of your root assumptions, and so you must deal with them as such. They represent, however, deep unities that you do not understand."[1]

If we can accept this new way of understanding the mysteries of God and His creation, we then can see evil and good as simply two opposites that together create a deeper unity, a completeness, of truth.[2] Perhaps this helps to solve the dilemma we had in our first essay in trying to understand how evil appeared in a supposedly perfect universe.

These concepts we have been grappling with in this essay are summed up beautifully in the words of Emmanuel[3]:

> *Evil is only ignorance*
> *of Divine Will and Divine Law*
> *None would resist God's Will*
> *if they were aware*
> *that it consists of their own joy,*
> *bliss and eternal happiness.*
>
> *Although the negative energies*
> *may seem not to flow with God's natural laws,*
> *they are indeed present in your physical world*
> *doing God's work.*
> *Without them, you would not be offered*

a choice between darkness and Light
and your growth process would be much hindered.
So, you see, they are a necessary ingredient.
These energies are not masters, they are servants
of God's Will . . .

---

[1]Jane Roberts, *Seth Speaks: The Eternal Validity of the Soul.* Prentice Hall Press, New York, 1972, p. 406.

[2]For a thorough discussion of this concept see Norman Friedman, *Bridging Science and Spirit.* Living Lake Books, St. Louis, Missouri, 1990.

[3]*Emmanuel's Book,* compiled by Pat Rodegast and Judith Stanton. Bantam Books, New York, 1985, p. 85.

✧ ⑥

The Separation

We have come to the dawning realization that God might not be separate from us but rather deep within us.

— Bishop Shelby Spong

As the reader knows, I was reared in a fundamentalist Christian home. My family and I attended the local Baptist church. Readers of a similar background can attest to the great number of sermons I was subjected to that warned us of hell-fire and damnation because of what Adam and Eve had done in the Garden of Eden. Because God had driven them out of the Garden, God had turned his face away from *me*, and I was doomed to eternal separation from Him unless . . . ! Unless I followed the prescribed ritual of publicly admitting my sin and asking Jesus to save me from God's wrath.

I heard those frightening sermons two times (sometimes even three times) on Sundays and once during the week. A few times a year we would attend revival meetings nightly for a week or more, meetings not only in our church but in other fundamentalist churches in our town or nearby towns, or even in large tents erected on an empty village lot or in someone's pasture.

Those visiting revival preachers really knew how to scare the devil out of me. Too, they were usually from a distant city and therefore special. Often they were advertised as ex-sinners of the worst kind. The more wicked they had been in their past, the more righteous they were purported to be now, and thus worthy of our rapt attention. Nobody really wanted to take the time to go to listen to someone who had been a goody-goody. My parents and neighbors wanted to live vicariously the sins of the preacher – the more sordid, the better.

Today, Christian ministers still speak of mankind's separation from his Creator. What do we really mean when we talk of separation from God? When did we become separated? Why did it happen? Did we ever consider that perhaps, just perhaps, God did not abandon us way back there in the Garden of Eden? Maybe our connection with God was never severed?

Before attempting to understand what the Separation really was, let us for a moment look at the historically accepted interpretation of the Separation by the Christian churches and some of its implications. According to the Christian scenario, Adam and Eve, created by God, were expelled from the Garden of Eden because they ate of the tree of knowledge. Since then, and because of that act, mankind has been conceived and born in sin. As a sinner one has need of salvation from eternal punishment in a hell of torment by a vengeful God. The Christian churches do not agree on the details of salvation, but generally agree that Jesus, as the only son of God, is the savior. The Christian accepts Jesus as savior and lord of his life. He worships Jesus as the only son of God and believes that the death of Jesus on the cross atoned for his sin. Accepting this, he then becomes reunited with God and the Separation is healed.

Assuming just for a moment that humanity is in need of salvation and that salvation is possible only through Jesus, why did God send Jesus to the Western world (the Greco-Roman world of his day)? Why were the people of the Roman Empire and, in particular, that rebellious corner of the Empire in the Middle East chosen for salvation and not the Chinese or the Africans or the natives of North America or even the peoples of the remote islands of the Pacific? Were these other peoples so sinful that they were totally unworthy? So sinful that they were beyond salvation? The gospel of Jesus has not to this day reached some of the more inaccessible places on the planet. Are these souls then lost for eternity? They are if the historically accepted idea of the Separation is true.

The principal implication of the Christian idea that mankind was separated from his creator in the Garden of Eden, of course, is that billions are forever lost from God. Lost forever are those from the past, those living in the present and those yet to be born (including billions who never heard of Jesus or the word "Christian," or even had the chance to hear a Jimmy Swaggart or an Oral Roberts on television). They are going to hell, to an everlasting punishment without hope of release from the unspeakable pain and torment of the place created by a vengeful God.

But let us go back to the beginning. Maybe we are *not* separated from God. Maybe we never were. Consider it: If we never were separated from our Creator, then we can, can we not, forget the entire scenario painted above? That would be incredibly wonderful, would it not? I'm sure that most readers would agree that it would indeed be wonderful if all peoples everywhere, past, present, and future, were and are sons and daughters of God and therefore heirs of God and heirs to all the promises of God to His children.

Unfortunately, I'm equally sure that some readers do not like such an idea. I can imagine some readers objecting violently and insisting that people are sinners, that they are vile creatures and deserve a hell. But did not Jesus say that the innocent one, the one without sin, should throw the first stone? Are we innocent? Are we, are you, ready to cast that first stone? Many of us take pride in our superiority, our supposed "chosen" status, being one of the elect! Some, I fear, actually take delight in "knowing" that certain people are going to hell!

I recall some folk within our church circle when I was growing up in Minnesota who, being exceptionally holy, seemed to really hate those in the community who were considered bad, those who drank beer in the local tavern, frequented the dance halls with their loose-living friends and seemed to be happy, easygoing folks. Even in my very young years I had the strong suspicion that my Christian friends despised these sinning folks because they seemed to actually enjoy life. Those "Christian" haters were serious, sober, seldom-smiling folk, always finding fault with others and proclaiming with great satisfaction that those who sinned certainly deserved their eternity in the flames with the devil. I, in my childish innocence, felt more friendly and warm toward those happy, carefree sinners than I did toward the self-righteous churchgoers.

If we never were separated from God, then it follows that we do not need a savior in the traditional Christian sense. We don't need to be saved. We are not in danger of going to a hell. We are, indeed, a son or daughter of God and joint heir with Jesus.

What, then, was the Separation of mankind from God all about? It was, I believe, false understanding on our part. In our guilt we thought that God had abandoned us. Did not God create us in His own image and likeness? That is, did not God create us out of light and energy just as God *is* light and energy? We are an extension of God, a part of God. We are divine beings of light and energy. Could God separate part of Himself from Himself? Jesus asks in *A Course in Miracles,* "Can you exclude yourself from the universe, or from God Who is the universe? I and my Father are one with you, for you are part of us. Do you really believe that part of God can be missing or lost to Him?"[1]

Yes, there was an event that took place that has come to be known as the Separation or the Fall, but in that event we were not abandoned by our Creator. It seems to me that we turned away from God, and after realizing what we had done, believed, because we felt somehow at fault, that the Spirit of God had left us. The Fall began before man was in physical form, while he was yet a pure energy spark or soul of God's creation. The entire planet earth was, I believe, the mythical Garden of Eden.

"In the beginning was the word." The "word," the breath of God, the cosmic energy of God, created the hierarchies of divine beings as defined in Genesis. These creative Rays of God fashioned the stars and galaxies and populated the planets and universes with His living creatures of all kinds, including the souls of mankind. Humanity was created as an extension of the Father, created as a spirit being of purity and beauty, a soul with a free will to choose – free even to turn his back on his Creator. After the battle between the Archangel Michael and the rebels, mankind turned his face away from the cosmic energy of God and toward the biblical Lucifer. This, it seems to me, was the Fall, or Separation, when the souls were beguiled by the "lies of the serpent" as recorded in Genesis. The souls were then encased in a physical body for their protection, to contain their spiritual light. Mankind, then, was destined to live out life in sweat and tears on his long journey back to the realization that he was still a child of God and that even though he had turned his back on God, God had not abandoned him.

Meister Eckhart, nearly seven hundred years ago, said it so beautifully, "God is at home. It is we who have gone out for a walk."[2] And as Emmanuel says it in our time[3]:

> The separation from God
> began a journey of Love.
> The individuating consciousness seeks
> to know itself fully and completely
> so that it can return to the Oneness. . .
>
> The prodigal son returns.
> In truth, one never "fell" at all.
> The Fall is a symbol of human experience.
> As a symbol it is the forgetting
> of the initial purpose of individuation,

getting lost in distraction,
the intent of the soul forgotten.
How could one leave God?
One is God.

For thousands of years we have experienced lives of toil and pain, lives of guilt, loneliness and despair, lives with the belief that God had abandoned us. We have debased ourselves and participated in all sorts of rituals, chanted innumerable liturgies and believed in all sorts of dogmas created by the wily priests and self-appointed power-mad, money-hungry religious authorities throughout the ages to appease the wrath of God. Millennium after millennium and century after century we have lived with the illusion of separation and desperately have sought deliverance from the bondage of sin.

Then Jesus came. Two thousand years ago Jesus was sent by God to this planet to remind us that we were and always have been a child of His. God had never abandoned us, Jesus taught. No longer would we need to be preoccupied with our dread of eternal punishment after we finished our earthly sojourn. But the message of Jesus, poorly understood by his disciples and by the religious leaders of the day, was turned into a new set of rituals, a new set of dogmas. A new religion was created, a religion *about* Jesus instead of the religion *of* Jesus.

Isn't it wonderful and liberating to know that we have not been abandoned by God and that we are and always have been His sons and daughters in whom He is well pleased?

---

[1] *A Course in Miracles, Text,* p. 180.

[2]Matthew Fox, *Meditations with Meister Eckhart.* Bear & Co., Santa Fe, New Mexico, p. 15.

[3]Pat Rodegast and Judith Stanton, compilers, *Emmanuel's Book,* p. 39.

✧ 7

The Cosmic Christ

I who am Divine am truly in you.
I can never be sundered from you:
However far we be parted, never can we be separated.
I am in you and you are in Me.
We could not be any closer.
We two are fused into one, poured into a single mold.
Thus, unwearied, we shall remain forever.

— Mechtild of Magdeburg
(ca. 1210 ca. 1280)

It is "time to move from the quest for the historical Jesus to the quest for the Cosmic Christ."[1] That is the thesis of Matthew Fox in his book *The Coming of the Cosmic* Christ. Fox, a Roman Catholic priest, is, of course, in deep trouble with the Vatican because of the ideas expressed in this and other works. He uses the scriptures in the work mentioned to show that the Cosmic Christ who lived in Jesus lives in each and every human who has ever walked this earth.

Every Bible student is familiar with the first chapter of John:

"In the beginning was the Word, the Word was with God and the Word was God. The same was in the beginning with God. . . . And the Word was made flesh and dwelt among us . . ." Christ existed before the beginning as the Word, or as consciousness or light, as the modern physicist would say (see Chapter 2). The Word was not only *with* God, the Word *was* God (recall our discussion of the hologram and the oneness of all). The Word (the light) became flesh in the person of Jesus. Jesus became the first full embodiment of the Christ. Each one of us has the Christ consciousness within (the soul), but we have not yet become fully aware of that fact. Jesus became aware that he was an extension of the Creator. He was fully aware that he was part of God.

It seems to me that Christianity (and most other religions) has become stagnant. It has become impotent. It has lost its real meaning and power to move the hearts of people. Christianity has become inflexible, unable to deal with scientific truths. It seems that the religious world would still like to believe that the world is flat, that this planet is the center of the universe and that mankind's history is only six thousand years old. Many Christians have become racist, prejudiced and bigoted, unable to fully accept all races, women, homosexuals and even the homeless as children of God equal to and one with all other children of God.

Christianity has become a set of rules and rituals, a set of dogmatic beliefs, the beliefs of tired old men wallowing in their traditions and enjoying their power. Christianity has become the religion *about* Jesus, not the religion *of* Jesus.

Also, it seems to me we have made an idol out of the Bible.

The Bible is still believed to be without error in every detail and to be literally true by the unquestioning Fundamentalist, in spite of many historical errors, obvious contradictions and additions and subtractions made in the original manuscripts. It's surprising how the fundamentalist Protestants accept the Bible blindly on faith when it was the Roman Catholic leaders of an earlier day who decided what was to remain and what was to be excluded from the Bible. The Christians of today must become aware that the canon left out great chunks of early scriptures because they didn't agree with Roman Catholic doctrines and traditions.

We have also, I believe, made an idol out of Jesus. Jesus came with a new gospel, the gospel of love, to make us aware of the Cosmic Christ within each of us. He did not ask or expect to be worshipped. He came as our elder brother, our wayshower. He did not come to establish yet another religion with a new set of dos and don'ts or to imprison us in new and better straitjackets. He came to set us free! Jesus says, "There is nothing about me that you cannot attain. I have nothing that does not come from God. The difference between us now is that I have nothing else. . . . I bridge the distance as an elder brother to you on the one hand, and as a Son of God on the other."[2]

We have even made idols out of our religious leaders — the Pope, infallible and imperious, for the Catholics; and the pastors and televangelists for the Protestants.

But how often our idols fall! The Jimmy Swaggarts and the Jim Bakkers seem to be everywhere. Will we ever learn? Will we stop sending them our dollars and putting our faith in them to do it for us? Is it not time to become aware of our own divinity, our own self-worth? Is it not time to become aware, as Meister Eckhart said so long ago, that we are God's sons and daughters? And is it not time to ponder what Matthew Fox (quoted at the beginning of this essay) said when he wrote that it is time to be less concerned about the historical Jesus and more aware of the presence of the Cosmic Christ within us?

I believe that the time has arrived when we as Christians, Jews, Moslems and followers of other religions are beginning to become aware of our true divinity. There is a worldwide surge of interest in spirituality (not religion). Witness, for example, the *New York Times* bestseller list. Books about angels, near-death experiences, reincarnation and other subjects of a metaphysical and spiritual nature are now appearing month after month in the top ten. Churches everywhere, even some within the most fundamentalist conferences, are beginning to preach tolerance, the acceptance of our neighbor as he is, and the recognition that each and every soul is on a spiritual path, a path leading to his/her becoming aware of the Cosmic Christ within — the path leading home.

---

[1]Matthew Fox, *The Coming of the Cosmic Christ.* Harper & Row, San Francisco, 1988, p. 7.

[2]*A Course in Miracles, Text,* p. 5.

✧ 8

Sin and Salvation

Be willing, then, to see your brother sinless, that Christ may rise before your vision and give you joy.

— from *A Course in Miracles*

Is there any subject dearer to the heart of Christians than the subject of sin and salvation? "Have you been saved? Have your sins been washed away? Are you born again?" Are these not the questions that a Christian directs to the stranger, to the visitor of his place of worship, to his fellow worker and to others he encounters on a daily basis? Having myself been brought up in a fundamentalist Baptist home, I am well-accustomed to such questions – directed to me and also directed by me to others.

All of mankind, each and every one of us, I feel, must admit to God and to ourselves that we are not always perfect in our actions and certainly not without malice in our thoughts toward one another (we are not always thinking loving thoughts). Yes, it seems to me, we have all "sinned" in both thought and action. Yes, we have all sinned against each other. And yes, some have even cursed our Creator. But are these wrong thoughts and actions sin? Consider this for a moment: Maybe we are not sinners.

Of course, it depends on how one defines sin. Before considering the literal meaning of the word (which is also the meaning given to it by St. Paul), let us look at the concept of sin as usually taught by both Protestant and Catholic Christians. Sin is a concept generally defined by Christians as any action, word or thought that separates them from God. In short, sin is anything that requires forgiveness and atonement.

If sin, as we have so far defined it, is what separates us from our God, perhaps we should question once again, as we have in other essays, *whether it is even possible* to become separated from our God. Did we become separated from the One who created us back at the "beginning" of time? Were we separated already at birth due to original sin, the consequence of Adam's sin? Can we become separated because of our individual shortcomings? In short, are we sinners? Are we really separate from our Creator?

Now let's look at sin in the more literal and biblical sense as defined by St. Paul. The word "sin" literally means "missing the mark." This is the meaning imparted to the word by the Gospels and by St. Paul. Sin is a failure on our part to be completely centered in God, to be imperfect in our words, actions and thoughts. As explained so beautifully and logically in *A Course in Miracles*, we humans condemn ourselves by our sinning, by missing the mark "of the high calling of God in Christ Jesus." God does not condemn us. We condemn ourselves. And if God doesn't condemn us, we do not need to ask Him for forgiveness, for He forgave us before we were born. He forgave us not for any sin we have committed (for it is impossible to sin in the sense of causing a separation), but He forgives us for forgetting who we are, for forgetting our divinity and for believing that we can successfully hide from Him in our ego bodies.

We, however, must forgive the world and everybody in it for all the wrongs that we have imagined done to us. *A Course in Miracles* says it this way: "When the thought of separation has been changed to one of true forgiveness, will the world be seen in quite another light; and one which leads to truth, where all the world must disappear and all its errors vanish."[1]

The core teaching of Jesus was to "repent and believe the Gospel" (Matt. 4:17). The Greek word, translated as "repent" in our Bible, is *metanoia,* which literally means "going beyond or higher than the mind." St. Paul defined it as the renewing of our mind in Christ. *Metanoia* is the state of consciousness where we transcend the ego with all of the hate, fear and selfishness that separate us from the true awareness of our divinity. Jesus said to love our enemies. When we learn to truly love all of creation, then we are beginning to transcend our ego and to be truly "born again."

Note that the ego and the human state of consciousness does not separate us from God, for that would not be possible, but it separates us from *knowing* that we are one with God. True repentance brings the awareness that the kingdom of God is within. The disciples one day asked Jesus where heaven was. Jesus answered by saying not to look up into the "heavens" for heaven. The kingdom of heaven, he said, was within them. In other words, heaven is the soul, the real me, the real you. So why do the preachers still talk about going to heaven when we die? Do they not read the scriptures? We *are* the kingdom of heaven! In *A Course in Miracles* Jesus says that if we ask where heaven or anything is, we just do not understand. There is no *where;* all is one. Also recall that Jesus said, "You are one with me as I am one with the Father" and in John 10:34 he reminded the disciples of their divinity by saying, "Is it not written in your law, I said, Ye are gods?"

In the most recent translation of the letters of Paul, the King James reading of Romans 3:9 is changed from "they are all under sin" to read "a disregard of the law." Paul then says, ". . . in universal terms, there is no such thing as sin. . . . Sin, the teaching of sin, is a means of coercion through fear."[2] Our Lord Jesus, overlighted by the Christ, demonstrated to us by his life, death and resurrection that all of God's creation will become perfected as he was, but it is each person's decision as to how and when that will happen.

Matthew Fox, in his book *Original Blessing,* demonstrates that the Fall/Redemption model of spirituality is not in the Bible and was not mentioned by any Christian writer before the life and writings of St. Augustine, a Catholic monk of medieval times who wrestled mightily with his own terrible pangs of guilt, particularly over his sexuality. Fox uses the term "creation spirituality" for what the scriptures teach in place of the Fall/Redemption model of St. Augustine and subsequent theology. It is interesting to note that although our universe is twenty billion years old, mankind in physical form has been here for only about four million years. According to the model of St. Augustine, sin entered the universe with the advent of mankind in a physical body (the Fall), which means that the universe was without sin for some 19,996,000,000 years!

The thesis of Fox, taken from the Old Testament, is that humanity was born with original blessing, not original sin. The Old Testament does not teach original sin. The Old Testament is the sacred book of the Jewish people. If original sin were taught there, the Jewish rabbis would certainly be aware of it. The great teacher, Rabbi Elie Wiesel, agrees, for he wrote that the idea of original sin was alien to Jewish tradition.

In *A Course in Miracles*[3] Jesus is quoted as saying that when you are tempted to believe in sin, you should remember this:

> If sin is real, both God and you are not. If creation is extension, the Creator must have extended Himself, and it is impossible that what is part of Him is totally unlike the rest. If sin is real, God must be at war with Himself. He must be split, and torn between good and evil; partly sane and partially insane. For He must have created what wills to destroy Him and has the power to do so. Is it not easier to believe that you have been mistaken than to believe in this?

What, then, about salvation? What is the atonement? Why did Jesus die on the cross for our "sins"?

According to the Bible, God is not willing that one soul be lost. Can one countermand God's will? *All will be saved!* Eventually each and every one of God's sons and daughters will be healed of the imagined separation and return to the awareness of who he or she is. Everyone is on a path back to this awareness, back to God. Some are on a more direct path than others, but none can be lost in the eternal sense. We are lost only in the sense that we have wandered off our path, taken all sorts of detours and gotten stuck for a time in the mire of the physical world's temptations and allurements. Many of us too have gotten lost in religion, in rituals and ceremonies, repeating endless prayers, believing that somebody or something outside of ourselves is necessary to save us from punishment or even annihilation.

When mankind accepted the idea of guilt, the idea of separation was born; and when he accepts the atonement, the idea of separation is ended. Guilt is what hides the face of Christ from us. I believe that God's son – each one of us – is blameless, guiltless. I believe that the atonement (at-one-ment) is mankind's final lesson, "for it teaches him that, never having sinned, he has no need of salvation. . . . That is why Atonement centers on the past, which is the source of separation, and where it must be undone. For separation must be corrected where it was made."[4]

Salvation, then, which eventually will come to every soul, however long it may take, is achieved when we recognize the guiltlessness of the son of God, each one of us recognizing our innocence. God created us; He knows what we are. He knows He created us out of Himself and that we remain within Him. He knows, as we will come to know, our guiltlessness. No one is without His holiness. No one is unworthy of His love.

The crucifixion showed that one can assault the body and even destroy it. But anything that can be assaulted or destroyed is not real (because the real world is as eternal as God Himself). It taught us that we (the real self, the soul) cannot be assaulted or destroyed, and through the resurrection we know that the spirit, the soul, is eternal.

Our resurrection is our reawakening. Jesus said, "I am the model for rebirth, but rebirth itself is merely the dawning on your mind of what is already in it. God placed it there Himself, and so it is true forever."[5]

A careful reading of the eighth chapter of Romans in its entirety is a good summary of all that has been written in this essay. I am using the latest translation of the letters of Paul.[6]

> There is now therefore no condemnation for anyone who believes and follows the truth which Jesus the Christ taught. All we who do this, follow not after the lesser self, but after the Spirit. It is the very truth of the law which the Christ in Jesus made manifest, that frees us all from the ways of the flesh, and eventual death. The law of itself could not do this, because it had been reduced to the terms of the lesser self. God sent His own Son to re-interpret the law, that its rightness might be once again seen and followed. When we interpret the universal laws through the Spirit, which is the higher self, then we can no longer interpret those same laws through the eyes of the lesser self. Unto all those who live by the higher laws, there is the promise of Life and Peace.
>
> The lesser self is at enmity with the higher laws of God. If, therefore, one follows only after the needs of the flesh, one cannot attain the things of the higher self or spiritual man. When once we recognize that the Divine dwells in each of us, then we are of Spirit. This was the very message of Christ, in whom we all now believe. When we begin to walk the path of Divinity, and accept the Inner

Christ, then we cease to attach so much importance to things of the flesh. The very Spirit that raised up Christ Jesus from the dead, dwells in each one of you. All those who accept this fact are equally Sons of God, and we may all call upon the name of God, even as did He. The Divine in each of us bears witness to the very fact that we are all equal, and joint heirs to the realms of Spirit. Even as He suffered and was glorified, so may we be glorified. Any suffering that we undertake on Earth is worthwhile for our progress toward Divinity. Although much that we undertake upon Earth is learned through suffering and travail, we shall set this as naught when we attain the perfection that Christ promised is possible for each of us.

We are encouraged by this truth in the just hope that we may each attain to His glory, through our continued efforts. Therefore, let us all work diligently and with patience upon that path. The spirit of each one of us makes intercession in those higher realms, and we know that all things work together towards a common good. Those who follow the heart, and who love one another and follow God may consider themselves as true followers of Divine Purpose. We are all predestined to follow in the footsteps of the Son of God who is the Christ.

What then might we say in consideration of all this? We need no longer fear, for when God is with us, nothing can be against us. Does not that same God who gave His own Son also give us all things freely? Only God, or the Divine in each of us can justify our actions. Who then can condemn us? Who shall separate us from the love of Christ? Shall we be daunted by any kind of tribulation, distress, persecution, famine, nakedness, or peril of any kind — even the sword? It is written that we must "die" to the lesser self daily, even as sheep for the slaughter. Yet in all of these things we are more than conquerors through Him that loved us. Through Him, I am persuaded that neither death, nor life, nor angels, nor principalities, nor powers, either present or to come, nor height or depth, nor any other being can separate us from the love of God which was demonstrated by the Christ in Jesus our Lord.

---

[1]*A Course in Miracles, Workbook for Students,* p. 403.

[2]Hilarion, *The Letters of Paul.* Triad Publishers, Ashland, Oregon, 1989, p. 31.

[3]*A Course in Miracles, Text,* p. 377.

[4]*Ibid.,* pp. 221, 331.

[5]*Ibid.,* p. 86.

[6]Hilarion, *op. cit.,* pp. 51-53.

The Wages of Sin

The wages of sin is death, but the gift of God is eternal life through Jesus, the Christ.

— Romans 6:23

I'm sure that many readers have heard dozens of sermons by their pastors using the verse quoted above as their principal text. Certainly, that text was frequently used in my days of coming of age in various Baptist and similar denominational churches. Today that passage is still one of my favorites. However, now I use it to point out a message very different from my earlier understanding – an understanding blindly accepted in my youthful days of unquestioning adherence to the religious views of my elders.

To you, the reader, what does that verse mean? What images do you visualize when you read those words of the apostle Paul? How many sermons have you heard based on that verse and other similar passages in the New Testament? How often have you endured with pain, as I have, the inflamed rhetoric of red-faced pastors and evangelists preaching on the wrath of God —a God, they say, who will turn you over to the charge of a devil who will hold you in his hell to be tormented forever and ever (the preacher all the while doing his very best to frighten you to "come forward and be saved," to be "born again")?

What does Romans 6:23 mean to the fundamentalist Christian? I think he would respond by saying that the verse means that if he commits sin he is condemned to a hell of eternal punishment by a wrathful God, but if he is born again and accepts Jesus as his personal savior he will gain eternal life. Is that about right? I believe that my readers will agree. Let's look at the verse more closely for a moment. Do we really see anything in that verse about a hell or a devil? Does it say anything about eternal punishment? Does it say anything about being condemned by a wrathful God? Do even the words "saved" or "born again" appear in that passage? The answer to all those questions is obviously no. Then perhaps we should stop and ask ourselves where those imaginative ideas came from.

I attended quite faithfully the Dean Street Baptist Church in Brooklyn, New York, for about two years in the sixties. The church was a small congregation of elderly Swedish folk and quite a few younger people, largely Hispanic. At that time I had resumed reading my Bible after an interim of a few years. I decided then to read them with an open mind, as much as possible giving up the interpretations with which I had been indoctrinated in my youth.

As I carefully read the New Testament, I slowly became aware that I hadn't come upon many of the concepts of my early training. So I started searching diligently for those missing concepts – they must be here someplace, I reasoned. Finally, frustrated in my search, I visited the pastor of the Dean Street flock. He was from what was then the Swedish Baptist Conference and a graduate of Bethel College and Seminary in St. Paul, Minnesota. (Incidentally, I had attended Bethel College for a year and a half before joining the Army Air Corps, and my brother had graduated from both the college and the seminary.)

I explained my unsuccessful search to find in my Bible a number of the teachings of the church. The pastor, visibly not exactly delighted with my questioning, responded with sincerity, saying that I couldn't find those ideas in the Bible because they were not there. He claimed that many of those biblical interpretations were largely the result of the teachings of Dr. Ironsides and other church leaders of the nineteenth and early twentieth century. Appreciating his honesty and frankness, I blurted out, "Why, then, don't you tell your congregation the truth?" His apologetic answer was that to his congregation and similar groups throughout Fundamentalism, the disputed doctrines that were not in the Bible were "more gospel than the Gospels," and if he proclaimed the truth on a Sunday morning he would be expelled from his position by Monday morning!

Yes, I do believe the wages of sin is death. Yes, I do believe that each and every one of us is sinful in our ego body, that is, we make all sorts of mistakes and therefore we will die – our body dies. The soul, the real you, the real me, was given the gift of eternal life through Christ who existed with the Father from the "beginning" and can never die. Eternal life was a gift from the beginning. We cannot earn it, we cannot lose it. God created us as perfect and eternal as He is Himself. Yes, I believe that if it were otherwise, God would not be God.

Consider carefully these words of Paul in Romans 6:11-23. The passage is from the latest English translation of his letters[1]:

> In a sense, we were all crucified with Christ, and we there-fore were all resurrected with Him. If we truly accept this, we can no longer carry on ignoring the truth. The message that Christ taught was that death has no domin-ion. It is said that the wages of sin is death but the gift of God is eternal life through Christ, our Lord. What this means is that all that we do, all of our actions, are accountable to the laws of cause and effect. Once we expiate that karmic responsibility and arrive at a time when we acknowledge the laws and live by them, we may also arrive at that point when we no longer fear death. We then acknowledge that the transition we call death is merely passage into another realm of existence which goes on into eternity.

I believe that the world we perceive is a world of separation. The physical world perceived by us through our five senses is a world not created by the First Cause, but is a world of illusion made by our split mind. "God so loved the world . . ." God does love the real world. Those who can perceive the real world can-not perceive this physical world, which is the symbol of death, or illusion. In the real world all is eternal — there is no death. If man *could* actually separate himself from the mind of God, he would certainly die.

It seems to me that the body does die as a consequence of

the "sins of the flesh," but you and I as souls are eternal, without beginning and without ending, as eternal and guiltless as our Creator of which we are part.

---

[1]Hilarion, *The Letters of Paul,* p. 41.

✧ 10

The Fear of the Lord

There is no fear in love; but perfect love casteth out fear: because fear hath torment. He that feareth is not made perfect in love.

— I John 4:18

"So-and-so is a God-fearing person." How often we hear such a statement. The thought, it seems, is that if a person fears God he or she is a moral, upright citizen, someone to be trusted, admired, loved. Do we fear God? *Should* we fear God? Do we *love* God? Do you believe that it is possible to truly love God and fear Him at the same time?

Man has only two basic emotions. According to psychologists the human psyche can experience only two basic feelings, those of love and fear. Fear includes all the negative emotions — hate, envy, jealousy, lust, anger, malice etc. For example, one cannot hate someone without fearing that person. A student might say that he hates his teacher. Why? Because he fears what his teacher may do to him. The student may fear embarrassment, humiliation, poor grades or just long, difficult work assignments.

As a child reared in a "God-fearing" Baptist home, on my bedroom wall hung a plaque with the puzzling words, "The fear of the Lord is the beginning of wisdom." Those words, seen every morning when I got up and every night before turning out the lamp, perplexed me greatly. I couldn't understand why I should fear God when everyone around me, my mother and father, my church pastor and Sunday school teachers, always taught me to love God. Even then, as a child, I realized that I couldn't do both. I couldn't really love God as long as I feared Him.

After many years of thinking about this perplexing problem it seemed at last clear to me why Christians, especially those in the more fundamentalist churches, fear God. And of course, if they fear God, they unconsciously hate Him. (Of course, they don't allow themselves to acknowledge the hate – or even to acknowledge the fear, for that matter.) The stories of the Old Testament God have been pounded into their minds and hearts. The reader of the Old Testament saw that God was "a wrathful and jealous" God, a God filled with unreasonable hate, a racist God filled with prejudice and one who showed no mercy. Yes, it seems very understandable why they could fear and therefore harbor hatred for that God. But how could one hope to truly love Him while still holding fear and harboring hate?

Most Christians believe that they are sinners, lost souls, and bound for an unspeakable eternal punishment unless saved from this wrathful, avenging God who will show them no mercy. This

God whom we are supposed to love is to be the very one to mete out the punishment. Ever since God allegedly threw us out of the Garden of Eden, we have run from Him, we have hid from Him because we fear His wrath. We fear and hate Him and look to someone to save us. We look to Jesus to intercede on our behalf to protect us from that wrathful God.

But what if the Bible never did say that the fear of God was the beginning of wisdom? Yes, the King James and most other English versions say just that, but the writer of that passage really wrote something quite different! The original Hebrew, correctly translated into English, reads, "To stand in awe of God is the beginning of wisdom."

"To stand in awe of." That's quite different, isn't it? To stand in awe of His omniscience, His omnipotence, His omnipresence, to be in awe of His love — that is not *fearing* our Creator. We cannot love God if we fear him, but we can truly love God when we stand in awe of Him.

In the introduction to *A Course in Miracles,* Jesus says that "the opposite of love is fear, but what is all-encompassing can have no opposite. . . . Nothing real can be threatened, nothing unreal exists. Herein lies the peace of God."

If God is love, only love, there is no room for an opposite. Fear is not part of the reality of God. Fear is part of the illusion of our reality while in a physical body living in time and space.

✧ 11

God's Blessing

"May God bless you." One hears it from nearly everyone and hears it often. It is only outdone by the obligatory and tiresome, "Have a nice day."

When a minister or priest finishes his sermon with the phrase, "May God bless you," we figure it gives a nice touch to the close of the service and think of his saying it as part of his job. In truth, however, when one says, "May God bless you," is one not being exceedingly arrogant? Is that not giving God permission to bless you? Do we really need to ask God for his blessing? *Should* we ask for His blessing? For ourselves? For others? Are we not God's sons and daughters, part of the sonship? Are we not one with God? Should we ask God to bless part of His own being?

One may argue that "may God bless you" is a nice-sounding phrase. It's harmless. It may even do good for many to hear the phrase spoken to them. Yes, all that may be true. But if so, then let's change the phrase to make it correct as well as well-meaning. How about, "May you be aware of God's blessing"? That speaks to the human condition. That speaks to the truth.

We always have God's blessing but are not always consciously aware of that fact. We cannot avoid His blessing, for "He maketh the sun to shine on the unjust as well as upon the just."

Perhaps if the parishioners were to hear each Sunday morning the phrase, "May you be aware of God's blessing," they might gradually become aware of all the great blessings they already have and always will have. They then, possibly, will begin to live happier and more fruitful lives.

✧ 12

The Love of God

God loves us. Yes, that is true, but . . .

When you think the thought, "God loves me," what picture
do you see in your mind? When the Christian preacher pro-
nounces the benediction with the words, "The Lord make his
face to shine upon thee and be gracious unto thee. The Lord
lift up His countenance upon thee, and give thee peace," what
do you visualize? I guess that most of us instinctinvely picture
a Moses-like figure smiling benevolently down upon us with great
love and compassion. But does God love? If God can show love
to us, does that leave open the possibility that He can occasion-
ally demonstrate to us something other than love? Are there
times when God withholds His love from us? Do we believe that
He loves the Christian more than the Moslem? More than the
atheist? Do we believe that He shows favoritism for the United
States over Russia or Iraq? I think not!

The Greeks, Romans and earlier peoples had what we have
patronizingly called anthropomorphic gods. But do we not also
make our God anthropomorphic? Do we not also make our God

into the likeness of man? Does not the benediction quoted above picture an anthropomorphic God? God is not an entity sitting on a throne dispensing love as He sees fit. God does not give His love to us. He does not *have* love to give. (If He *has* something, He *is* obviously something other than what He has.) God *is* love! The very essence or beingness of God is love. Only love. This "isness" of God, this love, envelops and surrounds us. In God we are completely immersed in an ocean of love. There is nothing else.

Yes, God is love. God is everything that is. Then is not everything love? All else is part of the illusion that we experience (enjoy? suffer? endure?) while in our ego bodies, the bodies that we have because of the guilt we feel once we believe we have become separated from our Creator.

So let us practice living *in* love, living *in* God. We can begin living in love, living in God, by realizing that because each of us is a son or daughter of God, we too are love. Let us love ourselves and each other and every one of God's creatures. The more we allow ourselves to sink into the ocean of love that we call God, the less fear we will have. Only by letting go of fear will we begin to demonstrate to our brothers and sisters the love of God.

The Will of God

There is no will but God's.

— from *A Course in Miracles*

"Thy will be done" we repeat in the Lord's Prayer. But we usually exercise our own will, do we not? What is God's will? What is our will? Are they different? Is it possible that any power or will can overturn the will of our omnipotent Creator? Could God's will and our will possibly be the same?

If we are an extension of God's essence, a very part of His being, one drop in the ocean of His love, can we have a will separate from His own? It doesn't seem possible, does it?

It seems that God's will and our will is the same. At our core is God and His will. What we actually do, however, is to succumb to our guilt and fear. Our ego and its will wins, and we listen and follow its dictates. Our deepest heartfelt wish yearns to realize our oneness with God, but our ego, ignorantly blackmailing us with guilt, causes us to succumb to its will. The ego, part of the illusion of our physical existence, will in time be defeated as we listen more to the Holy Spirit, that part of the oneness of God that communicates to us from within.

Complete peace and joy in our life is God's will for us. As long as we do not have that perfect peace and joy, we are not acknowledging God's will in our life. We do not acknowledge His will because we are not fully aware that we are one with Him. When we recognize ourselves for what we truly are, then we will recognize God and His will for us. We will know oneness with our Creator when we understand that there is no separation between His will and our will.

In our daily living in this physical earthly plane we follow the wishes and the will of the ego, but those are the wishes of a part of us that truly does not exist in reality, being part of the illusion of living in time.

Jesus tells us to leave the sins of the ego to him. That is what the atonement is for. Only the ego can experience the feeling of guilt, and as long as we feel guilt, the ego is in control. When we can see the sinlessness of the son of God (each one of us), then the atonement can release us from all guilt and we will know the will of God.

Our daily prayer should be to become aware of our divinity, to become aware of our oneness with Christ, our oneness with the Father, and to truly ask that His will be done in our life.

Sexuality

In the moment of your creation, you were given incredible gifts; and one of the most important is the gift of sexuality!
— Bartholomew

I can well imagine that many casual readers (especially bookstore browsers) have turned to this essay first — irresistibly drawn to it by the hint of something forbidden or erotic. Why are we so titillated by the subject of sex?

There are those who find every reference to sex, or even any slightly revealing photograph, obscene or dirty, something to avoid. Often, however, those same persons go out of their way looking for the obscene so they can register their objection to it. Such as the man who wrote a letter to the editor of one of the major daily newspapers in which he indicated that he had taken great offense to a picture of a little girl published earlier in that paper. He claimed that the photograph had revealed a small part of the girl's genital area. He discovered that fact, he said, by scrutinizing the photo with a magnifying glass!

There are those who greatly enjoy telling off-color, sexually oriented jokes. These are often the same persons who verbally or sexually abuse others and/or the ones who brazenly leer or make obscene gestures to impress their peers.

Why are we in the Western world, especially those of us in the United States, so obsessed with sex?

The Christian believes, along with those of other faiths, that God made humans male and female, endowing them with sexual organs. Therefore He certainly intended that male and female come together physically and be as one. The fact that we are sexual beings is perfectly natural and normal. Why, then, do we snicker when we hear about a friend's sexual improprieties? Why, then, do we enjoy the lurid stories of the sexual lives of the rich and famous? Why are we so embarrassed about sex that we cannot teach our children about it? Why are so many of us afraid of sex education in our schools?

Is it guilt? Many, perhaps most of us, feel guilty about having sexual feelings. We feel even more guilty and sinful when we give in to those feelings. Why is there rape, incest and sexual abuse of children? I believe it is because we are overridden with guilt due to our Judeo-Christian heritage. Our whole society is immersed in the taboos of the Old Testament, those taboos of the Hebrews written to ensure for them a large progeny for military fodder – for their security and victory over their enemies during their wandering in the wilderness. I believe that the unconscious mind of Western culture has been seared with guilt about its sexuality. The rest of the world experiences this guilt also, but perhaps less so.

Guilt has caused many people to repress their sexual instincts in the attempt to conform to the laws and mores of their parents, their church and society in general. Some people, when they no longer can suppress their feelings or conform to the dictates of society, commit rape, child abuse, incest etc. Or, as in the case of teenage homosexuals, they commit suicide. What would happen if all laws regulating sex were abolished?

Bartholomew, channeled by Mary Margaret Moore, suggests just that. Most readers, I imagine, would express horror at such a development, believing that man would become uncontrolled in his passions and "become some kind of sexual beast"[1] as Bartholomew says it. But he argues, and I agree, that the opposite would happen: that an awareness within us would regulate our sexuality much better than any law ever has or ever could. Seth enthusiastically agrees when he says, "Many of you are afraid that without a feeling of guilt there would be no inner discipline, and the world would run wild. It is running quite wild now – not despite your ideas of guilt and punishment, but largely because of them."[2]

So it seems that all the laws throughout the world have not deterred man from seeking sexual satisfaction, whether it be legal in his particular society or not.

As an example, let us consider the subject of homosexuality. Homosexuality has been considered an abomination by the Judeo-Christian world. In most other societies it has been understood somewhat better and accepted more freely. Hopefully, with new scientific evidence linking the inclination toward same-sex relationships with genetics, people will learn to be more tolerant. But why the intolerance in the first place? It is generally agreed that approximately one-sixth of the world's population is homosexual or strongly bisexual.[3] This is as true today as it has been in all past historical periods and all societies or cultures of which we have knowledge.

What is perversion? Is it not perversion when one goes contrary to his or her own nature? If it is one's nature to find sexual satisfaction in the opposite sex, then it would be an act of perversion to have a sexual relationship with a member of your own sex. If it is one's nature to find true love and satisfaction only from one's own sex, then it would be a perversion to have a sexual relationship with a member of the opposite sex. Jason suggests that each person should make his own choice and not let society impose a particular expression of sexuality. He says, "Be free, then, to make choices of male and female, male and male, or female and female according to what is truly your preference . . ."[4]

Bartholomew says much the same when he declares that each of us must do what makes us feel creative, loving and positive, because if we attempt to follow the codes of our society against our nature, we will become confused and conflicted in our emotional and spiritual life, ending up angry, resentful and judgmental. He adds, "You believe that God cares in the most minute detail what you do with your sexuality. But He doesn't care. That is your business . . . He has only one concern, and that is the quality of your awareness, your power, your love, and your compassion."[5]

Today's fundamentalist Christians, especially those who fol-

low Pat Robertson, Jerry Falwell and others of the extreme political right wing, single out for their denunciation anything that
seems to them to be sins of the flesh. For example, they love to
condemn homosexuals to the "fires of hell." They excuse their
contempt and hatred of the homosexual by their interpretation
of certain passages, especially those from the Book of Leviticus.
They seem to be adept at overlooking other passages of the Old
Testament (many of which are also in Leviticus) that equally pro-
hibit and condemn sexual acts the heterosexual is more likely to
commit. One who commits adultery is condemned, and one
who commits onanism is sentenced to *death*. It is hard to believe
that was the punishment for simply spilling one's seed upon the
ground. I would guess that every man is guilty of that one!

Those religious leaders who self-righteously condemn those
who have loving relationships different from those they themselves have are just continuing the age-old conspiracy against
individual freedom. Since almost the beginning of man's sojourn
on this planet there has been a conspiracy of distortion and lies
to make man feel guilty about his sexuality. Both political and
religious leaders have fostered the idea of human guilt and continue to try to expand their control thereby. Barbara Marciniak's
source, in her channeled book *Bringers of the Dawn,* says[6]:

> The orgasm has been distorted from its original purpose.
> Your body has forgotten the cosmic orgasm of which it
> is capable because society has taught you for thousands
> and thousands of years that sexuality is bad. You have
> been taught this in order for you to be controlled and to
> keep you from seeking the freedom available through sex-

> uality. Sexuality connects you with a frequency of ecstasy, which connects you back to your divine source and to information.

Sexuality was given to mankind as a great gift from God. Through the sexual experience we can discover our true being, we can discover who we are. In our sexual experience we become one with another human, but we are in actuality seeking unity with God. If we did not have all of that guilt in our sexual relationships we would more truly experience, in the coming together with the one we love, the oneness of all; we would become aware of the fact that we truly are a son or daughter of the Creator and that we are indeed one with God.

I do not believe that God judges us on the level of our sexuality. God is only interested in the level of our love, in the level of our understanding. In God there is neither male nor female. There is only one God, of which every one of us is a part.

I believe that in the remaining few years of this century we will clear out the negativities of our understanding of our sexuality and understand that the sexual coming together of two in an act of love is one sure way of connecting to our higher self and to our Creator.

---

[1]Bartholomew, *I Come as a Brother*. High Mesa Press, Taos, New Mexico, 1986, p.23.

[2]Jane Roberts, *The Nature of Personal Reality*. Prentice Hall, Englewood Cliffs, New Jersey, 1974, p. 68.

[3]Jess Stearn, *The Sixth Man*. Doubleday & Co., New York, 1961.

[4]Ron Goettsche and Bob Fogg, *Down to Earth*. Synergy Publishers,

Denver, Colorado, 1984, p. 52.

[5]Bartholomew, *op. cit.*, p. 22.

[6]Barbara Marciniak, *Bringers of the Dawn.* Bear & Co., Santa Fe, New Mexico, 1992, p. 211.

"I Am the Light of the World"

One of the lessons in *A Course in Miracles* has the student say: "I am the light of the world. That is my only function. That is why I am here."

Are we arrogant when we declare such a statement? I imagine that most readers would answer yes.

But who is the "light of the world" if it is not God's sons and daughters? And who are God's sons and daughters? I am. You are. Thus saying, "I am the light of the world" is simply declaring a fact. The statement is just the opposite of arrogance, the opposite of pride or self-deception. It is merely referring to oneself as we were created by God, created in His own image and likeness. It is a statement of true humility, recognizing the function that God assigned to us.

The Word of God

*But one does not eat out of a garden that grew in centuries
past.*

— Ken Carey

To most of my readers, perhaps, the Holy Bible is the only
true word of God. To others it may be the Koran or the Book
of Mormon or some other holy writing. Whichever it is for you,
you may believe that it is the *only* true word of God and consider other holy books to be less worthy, perhaps thinking of
them as evil, even the very words of Satan. But did you ever stop
to think why you accept that writing as the true word of God?
Did you not choose your holy scriptures because of the accident
of your birth — the country in which you were born, the ethnic
background of your family and the religious training given you
as a youth?

I would guess that many of my readers, and certainly most
Christians, believe the Holy Bible to be the only true word of
God. But is it the Old Testament, the New Testament or both?

The Jewish nation (Jews throughout the world) accepts the Old Testament but not the New Testament; the Christians accept both the Old and the New Testaments, with emphasis on the latter. The two testaments do indeed seem to be describing two different deities. The Old Testament God's behavior is jealous, racist, violent and antifeminist, whereas the God of the New Testament reflects compassion and love (see Chapter 20, "The God of the Old Testament").

God spoke to the Israelites through Abraham, Moses and the prophets. To the generations that followed, the words received by the earlier leaders and recorded in the Old Testament became the "word of God." God had spoken. It was His final word, His final law, the last instructions of the Creator to His creation.

Then Jesus came. His followers recorded the story of his life and his teachings as best they could remember and understand. Thus the New Testament became *the* word of God to the Christian. It contained, for them, the final pronouncements from their Creator.

Moslems accept Jesus and his teachings, but believe that the words given to Mohammed are the final inspired writings to humanity. The Mormons also accept the New Testament, but claim that the words received by Joseph Smith are the definitive word of God. Other religions, too, have their "word of God."

The various holy scriptures that we have mentioned and those of still other groups in other parts of the world were transcribed by people believed to be inspired by the Holy Spirit and were meant for those of their day. They were written in the framework of their current understanding of the workings of the cosmos and humanity's place in it.

What about today? Is God no longer interested in mankind and what happens to him on this planet? Is God no longer communicating to us? Has He forsaken us? I do not believe He has.

God is now speaking, it seems to me, as never before to the peoples of this earth, bringing the teachings of love to a higher octave of understanding. Jesus, as he told his disciples, could only speak in parables because of their lack of understanding. Today, in the late twentieth century, humanity has a much more enlightened understanding of its place and purpose in the cosmos and is ready to receive divine truths of a higher order.

I believe that God is speaking to people all over the world —to the Jew, to the Christian, to the Moslem, to those of all faiths and to those of no faith. To many, His truths are heard in subtle ways, the receiver never guessing from where his ideas, his thoughts, his revelations are coming. God is whispering to us through the trees, the wind, the mountains. God is speaking to us through the words of a stranger, the look of a child, a photo in a newspaper. What do we hear when we sit quietly by a gently flowing stream and meditate? What inspiration of peace and harmony do we feel when we gaze upon the distant mountains and watch at sunset the colors imperceptibly change from pink to crimson to dark blue and purple?

To many others, God is speaking more directly through the process commonly called channeling. There are a great number of incredibly beautiful and inspired writings transcribed by God-loving souls from dictations given them by the Holy Spirit. (The word "inspired" means "in the spirit.") These inspired channeled writings themselves tell us that this phenomenon will increase for a period, but become unnecessary when very soon each of us will be receptive directly to the promptings and teachings of the "word of God."

✧ 17

Jesus

Is he the Christ? O yes, along with you.
— from *A Course in Miracles*

Jesus Christ. As unbelievable as it may seem to most readers, there are many Christians who think that "Christ" is the last
name of Jesus! Most of my readers, I'm sure, are aware that
"Christ" is a title. It is correctly "Jesus, the Christ" or "the Christ,
Jesus." This idea is expressed clearly in the following passage[1]
in *A Course in Miracles*.

> The name of *Jesus* is the name of one who was a man but
> saw the face of Christ in all his brothers and remembered
> God. So he became identified with *Christ*, a man no
> longer, but at one with God. . . . Jesus remains a Savior
> because he saw the false without accepting it as true. And
> Christ needed his form [the physical body] that He might
> appear to men and save them from their own illusions.

Jesus, I believe, is our elder brother, our wayshower, the
lamp unto our feet and the light upon our path. I do not believe

that he wanted us to make an idol of him or to worship him. I believe that he came to teach us to become aware of our own divinity, to help us realize that we are all God's sons and daughters. I do not believe that he intended to start a new religion, to institute a set of rules or to introduce ritualistic practices in his name. Did not Jesus tell us that we would not only equal his "miracles" but do even greater things than he did?

Jesus was no different from the rest of mankind except in time. The entity Jesus went through the illusion of separateness from his Father, as we all have, but was the first to fully awake from that illusion. He was the first to fully realize his complete identity with Christ. "In the beginning was the word [Christ] . . . and became flesh and dwelt among us."

Jesus completed the atonement (at-one-ment). He completely overcame guilt and fear (separation). He had only the mind of Christ. As Paul said in Philippians 2:5, "Let this mind be in you, which was also in Christ Jesus," and in Romans 12:2, "Conform not to the world, but be ye transformed by the renewing of your mind."

Was Jesus born of a virgin? The virgin birth, perhaps, is one of the most sacred of beliefs in all of Christendom. To even question this belief is sacrilege to most believers. To question the virgin birth places one in danger of hellfire in many minds. I have, until recently, always accepted the teaching of the virgin birth. But now I question it. It certainly is possible that the teaching is true, but I feel now that it makes our relationship with Jesus very different from the one he wants with us.

First, there is absolutely nothing in the Bible that indicates a virgin birth. Yes, our King James version and most other English versions of the Bible use the word "virgin," but the original scriptures, translated correctly, give the phrase "a young woman." Second, and more important, it seems necessary to me that Jesus had a normal conception. Consider this: If the conception of Jesus was anything other than normal, having both a physical father and a physical mother, his message to us would be entirely meaningless, would it not? He came to show us that he was a "son of man" *as we all are* (in our physical bodies) and that we can all become fully Christed as he did. If he had been born in some supernatural way, that would mean that we could not follow his example. Jesus became what we all must become. His crucifixion demonstrated to us that God's son cannot be killed and that evil, guilt, fear and even death can have no power over us.

We have made a mockery of the life and teachings of Jesus. We have corrupted his message of love and forgiveness. We have allowed the ecclesiastics to pervert our understanding of his words. In short, we have made a new religion about and around Jesus, but have ignored his true teachings. We worship him instead of following in his footsteps. Ralph Waldo Emerson wrote, "Is it not time to present this matter of Christianity exactly as it is, to take away all false reverence for Jesus and not mistake the stream for the source?"[2]

Thomas Jefferson, the author of the Declaration of Independence and our third President, was dismayed when he realized that the New Testament account of Jesus had been tampered with by additions and subtractions. In a letter to Dr. Benjamin Rush, he wrote, "To the corruption of Christianity, I am, indeed, opposed; but not to the genuine precepts of Jesus himself. I am a Christian in the only sense in which he wanted anyone to be: sincerely attached to his doctrines in preference to all others, ascribing himself to every human excellence; and believing he never claimed any other."[3]

Jesus is our link back to God, back to the realization that we never left God. He is "the way, the truth and the life." To become a fully realized Christ is the way, the truth and life eternal. The body dies, the son of God is eternal. His sinlessness pictures our own.

As the living Jesus says, "You are already the Christ consciousness, dear ones; you've simply forgotten. The Christ is the full circle of light which exists in the hearts of all who love our Parent."[4] Yes, Jesus lives on. He is not dead. Yes, the physical body that Jesus used on earth is no longer needed, but Jesus continues his leadership role today. He is still the coordinator of God's workers on this planet. He is still our model and example and our Lord, one to go to in prayer for guidance and help in our walk on our path back to God, back to the awareness that we are one with Him.

---

[1]*A Course in Miracles, Manual,* p. 83.

[2]Quoted in Steven Mitchell, *The Gospel According to Jesus.* Harper Collins, New York, 1991, p. 17.

[3]*Ibid.,* p. 5.

[4]Virginia Essene, *New Teachings for an Awakening Humanity.* S.E.E. Publishing Co., Santa Clara, California, 1986, p. 128.

✧ 18

A Story of a Past Life

"You are coming home." These words seemed to come from someplace within me. The words made no sense to me. I was in a military aircraft approaching Capodoccino Airfield in Naples, Italy. It was 1945. I had never been out of the U.S. before and now a voice inside of my head was saying that I was coming home. The idea was so preposterous that I dismissed it. When the words came, I had been looking out the window at a hillside covered with umbrella pine trees. Seeing the trees, my stomach churned with inexplicable emotion. Then I remembered my high school Latin text with the photo of the Appian Way near Rome with umbrella pines bordering the road. I recalled looking at that picture many times for hours on end and experiencing strange emotions, almost seeing a picture in my mind or remembering something (but what?) for a split second. Now I was seeing trees like those in that picture. But why did this place affect me so compellingly?

I fell in love, one might say, with Italy and its people. At one level, an unconscious level, I knew somehow that I had been there before. I felt completely at home, especially in Rome, where, even though I was there for the first time, I knew the old parts of the city as if I had always been there. My heart pounded with excitement walking the Roman Forum and other ancient sites. I didn't understand why. I dismissed the feeling as another strange experience. I had heard, of course, of reincarnation, but never seriously considered it or even thought about it. I remembered the plaque on my bedroom wall as a kid, "Only one life, 'twill soon be past; only what's done for Christ will last!"

It was 1964. I was with two or three fellow teachers in a lower hallway at Horace Mann School in Riverdale, in the Bronx. It was my first day. While chatting with these new friends from the history department (I was to teach ancient history), a man walked by, a teacher from another department whom I had not yet met. As he passed by I became visibly agitated, to the point that my colleagues expressed concern. As the person passed I had heard a voice within me saying, "There goes your old friend, Savonarola." As with the voice years earlier in Naples, the words were disconcerting. But this time I did not simply dismiss them. By that time in my life I had been reading about Edgar Cayce and reincarnation and other spiritual concepts. So I pondered the meaning of the words.

A few days later, after I had made the acquaintance of the teacher who had passed in the hallway, I asked him whether he believed in reincarnation. His answer was, "No, of course not." "But Bob," I asked him, "If you had lived before, who would you have been?" Somehow I knew with absolute certainty how he would answer. He replied, "That's an easy question. I was Savonarola, of course. I always think of myself as Savonarola." Then I told him that my master's thesis at Columbia University, where I had just graduated the prior spring, was titled *The Martyrdom of Savonarola*. He became very excited, invited me to his classroom, told me to close the door and look behind it. There, hanging on the door, was a large portrait of Savonarola! My head was spinning, my heart was pounding!

A few years later I and other Americans were on a summer expedition to Cadiz, Spain, including a group of ancient history scholars and a number of young ocean divers from California. One day a member of the group, a celebrated psychic from California, meeting alone with me, went into a trance and proceeded to tell me about a life in Florence, Italy, in the late fifteenth century where, she said, I had known personally the famous preaching monk Savonarola! The psychic claimed that she had never heard of Savonarola nor did she know anything of the history of Florence during the Renaissance period.

When I had attended the University of Florence during the summer of 1947, I had been especially interested in the history of the period of Lorenzo the Magnificent and his protagonist, Savonarola. The statue of Savonarola, standing on the spot where he had been burned at the stake, had inspired an unforgettable emotional response. I imagine that was in part responsible for my choosing his life as the subject of my thesis.

What does one do with such a series of events? Ignore it? It would be rather difficult to dismiss such experiences as meaningless. I can hear a few of my readers saying that it must have been Satan trying to mislead or confuse me! Could it not more likely have been the spirit of God leading me? For me, those events plus other similar happenings led me to seriously consider the idea of reincarnation. Now, after years of study and thought, when someone asks, "Do you believe in reincarnation?" I answer, "No, I don't *believe* in it. I know for a fact that it is true."

✧ 19

On Reincarnation

I hold that when a person dies
His soul returns again to earth;
Arrayed in some new fresh-disguise,
Another mother gives him birth.
With sturdier limbs and brighter brain
The old soul takes the road again.

— John Masefield

Voltaire, who did not believe in the teachings of the Church but certainly was no atheist, as generally believed, asked of skeptics whether it would be more difficult to be born a second time than to be born once. Do you, my reader, feel that it is any more preposterous to believe that we have lived before birth than to believe that we will live after death? Can we truly explain the miracle of birth? Can we explain the miracle of life after death of the body?

If we cannot explain these miracles, why do we insist that it is impossible to have had a physical life or lives before our present one? By far the majority of people on earth believe in such prior existences. Among the nations of the world, we in the United States have one of the smallest number of believers, but according to a 1981 Gallup Poll twenty-three percent of Americans then believed in reincarnation, almost a quarter of our population. Twenty-five percent of Catholics and a surprising twenty-one percent of Baptists believed in reincarnation! The number of those accepting the idea of past lives is, I believe, growing very rapidly in the United States as well as throughout the West. I strongly suspect that many of my readers are turning to that understanding also.

An understanding of, or belief in, the idea of reincarnation is not necessary, of course. Actually, it may not even be very important. However, in my experience and in the experience of many others, understanding the concept of prior lives answers many puzzling questions and is a great help in accepting, appreciating and enjoying the problems and opportunities of the present. It gives one a fuller appreciation of the greatness of our God and His creation. After our imagined separation from our Creator, He allows us to come back repeatedly into a physical body until we finally get it right, until we come to the realization and remembrance that God is still our God and that we are still His sons and daughters. Then we will be ready to move on to a higher plane to be with the heavenly hosts and all of the "saints" who have preceded us.

Historically, it is quite difficult to find a name among the famous who did not believe in life before birth as well as life after death: Plato, Aristotle, Caesar, Shakespeare, Milton, Benjamin Franklin, Ralph Waldo Emerson, Walt Whitman, Thomas Edison,

Luther Burbank, George Bernard Shaw, Rudolf Steiner, Henry Ford, Rudyard Kipling, Mahatma Gandhi, Sir Winston Churchill and Charles Lindbergh, to name a few who believed and wrote about reincarnation. Many readers are probably saying, "So what? What other people have said or believed, regardless how many there have been or who they were, does not mean that the concept is a true one or that one must believe in it." True. Let me add just one more name: Jesus of Nazareth!

Adding the name of Jesus to those who understood and taught reincarnation may be surprising to you; it may even be inconceivable to many of you. But for those of you who are well acquainted with the historical period in which Jesus lived and are aware of the philosophical understanding of the religious communities of the Holy Land of those days, it is not surprising at all. Serious students of that part of the world and of that historical era will recall that especially the Essenes, the cultural and religious group from which Jesus came, were fully conversant with the ideas of many lives on the earthly plane.

Before we look at the words of Jesus on the subject, let us take a brief look at the concept of reincarnation in Judaism. The Old Testament neither denies nor proclaims rebirth of the soul, but in the Judaic tradition there is a strong indication of belief in the idea of a soul making many trips to this world before acquiring the perfection and experience needed to go on. The tradition teaches that Adam became, in turn, Seth, Noah, Abraham and Moses. We quote many pages to show the acceptance and understanding of reincarnation among the Jews, but to briefly demonstrate this, we will quote the Hasidic teacher Rabbi

Shneur Azlman, who wrote the following[1] "Prayer Before Retiring at Night."

> Master of the universe! I hereby forgive anyone who has angered or vexed me, or sinned against me, either physically or financially against my honor or anything else that is mine, whether accidentally or intentionally, inadvertently or deliberately, by speech or by deed, in this incarnation or in any other.

The Old Testament of the Christian Bible ended with the prophecy, "Look, I will send you the prophet Elijah before the great and terrible day of the Lord comes" (Malachi 4:5). As we will see later, Elijah was born in his new body as John the Baptist.

In Matthew 16:13-14 Jesus, in speaking to his disciples, indicates that belief in reincarnation is understood and accepted by his contemporaries:

> When Jesus came into the coasts of Caesarea Philippi, he asked his disciples, saying, Whom do men say that I the Son of Man am? And they said, Some say that thou art John the Baptist; some, Elias; and others Jeremias, or one of the prophets.

Then in Matthew 17:9-13 Jesus tells his disciples that Elijah has been reincarnated into a new body, that of John the Baptist:

> And as they came down from the mountain, Jesus charged them, saying, Tell the vision to no man, until the Son of Man be risen again from the dead. And his disciples asked him, saying, Why then say the scribes that

Elias must first come? And Jesus answered and said unto them, Elias truly shall first come, and restore all things. But I say unto you, That Elias is come already, and they knew him not, but have done unto him what they willed. Likewise shall also the Son of Man suffer of them. Then the disciples understood that he spoke unto them of John the Baptist.

This was stated even more emphatically by Jesus in Matthew 11:13-15: "For all the prophets and the Law foretold things to come until John appeared, and John is the destined Elijah, if you will but accept it. If you have ears, then hear."

It is easy for a student of the scriptures to see that the Jews of Jesus' day understood and accepted the concept of reincarnation of the soul. It is also obvious from other scriptures that Jesus took for granted the idea of reincarnation. For example, in Mark 10:29-31 Jesus speaks of more than one earthly life:

There is no man that hath left house, or brethren or sisters, or father, or mother . . . for my sake, and the gospel's, but he shall receive an hundredfold now in this time, houses, and brethren, and sisters, and mothers, and children, and lands, with persecutions; and in the world to come eternal life. But many that are first shall be last; and the last first.

Could all this have happened in that one lifetime, in one incarnation? Verse 31 above could be better translated to read, "But many that are first in this incarnation shall be last or in lowly positions in the next rebirth; while the last or least esteemed may be first in their future life."

In light of the fact that reincarnation was an accepted belief in Judea at the time of Jesus, it is odd, is it not, that reincarnation is considered a diabolical concept by many Christian fundamentalists when neither Jesus nor the gospel writers condemned it! Conversely, you might ask why the gospels and epistles of the New Testament do not have more to say about the subject if it were an accepted belief. The writers of the New Testament were not at all concerned about another earthly life because they were expecting the imminent end of the age and the reappearance of Jesus. After all, had not Jesus told them in Matthew 24:34, "The present generation will live to see it all"? And in Luke 21:32-33, "I tell you this: The present generation will live to see it all. Heaven and earth will pass away; my words will never pass away." Finally, at the end of Revelation he says, "Yes, I am coming soon" (Rev. 22:20). It matters not how we wish to interpret those scriptures now. At that time the hearers of Jesus' words believed that it referred to their day.

I believe that Jesus came to this earth two thousand years ago to plant the seeds of understanding. Those seeds are now reaching maturity after a slow germination and growing process for the last two millennia. He had told his disciples that they were not yet ready to understand many things (John 16:12-13) and that he spoke in parables to the multitudes so that they "may look and look but see nothing: they may hear and hear, but understand nothing." Then, in I Corinthians 3:1-4, Paul has this to say:

> For my part, my brothers, I could not speak to you as I should speak to people who have the Spirit. I had to deal with you on the merely natural plane, as infants in Christ.

And so I gave you milk to drink, instead of solid food for which you were not yet ready. Indeed, you are still not ready for it, for you are still on the merely natural plane.

Many of the secret teachings of Jesus given to his disciples were recorded in early writings. Some of these texts were called the Gnostic Gospels, based on the Greek word "gnosis," meaning "knowledge." Until being declared heretical and sought out and destroyed, these texts were considered of equal worth and of equal truth alongside the New Testament texts with which we are familiar. A copy of these Gnostic writings was buried in Upper Egypt by Coptic Christians to save them from the book-burning by the priests. In 1945 a peasant, while digging in his fields, discovered a large earthenware pot containing ancient papyrus texts (the Nag Hammadi Scrolls), which have proven to be the long-lost and long-sought-after Gnostic Gospels.

These texts, which add a great deal of knowledge to the story of the life and teachings of Jesus, emphasize the purpose of the coming of Jesus as the light of the world. They clearly teach that each person is part of the sonship, that each of us is a son or daughter of God and that man does not need an organized church or a priest to "save" him, for man was never lost. From a reading of these gospels it is easy to understand why the early church leaders felt compelled to suppress the Gnostic truths.

The early church, growing ever more influential within the Roman Empire, emphasized those writings that seemed to give the priests and bishops strong control and that did not conflict strongly with Roman rule. In the early fourth century, Constantine, the Roman emperor, found it to his advantage to convert to Christianity. Thus the Roman state gave political power and prestige to the growing influence of the church. In 313 A.D. Constantine made Christianity legal within the Empire, and in 324 A.D. it was given a specially favored position, thus creating a monolithic power that would continue to expand even after the defeat of the Roman Empire as a military-political power in the latter fifth century.

In 325 A.D., at the Council of Nicea, which was under the control of Constantine, the dangerous concepts of Gnosticism, including the belief in reincarnation, were no longer accepted as dogma. Finally, in the year 553 A.D., at the Fifth Ecumenical Council, these dangerous truths were declared anathema and expunged from the scriptures. It was largely a political decision. The Western Roman Empire was already in complete collapse, and it was becoming increasingly difficult to hold back the barbarians to the east. The Eastern Empire could not tolerate any further dissension in its midst. The leaders of the Empire as well as of the Church needed to have a hell, a heaven, and a judgment day to create an atmosphere of fear and submission in order to maintain their control. The Gnostic ideas of the divinity of man, equality of women within the church, reincarnation etc. threatened the order of the state and supremacy of the Church. Thus religious dogmas, rules and rituals were more firmly enforced to maintain their sure control of the masses.

Later, in the late Middle Ages, the Church found it necessary once again to deal with the issue of reincarnation. This time it was the Cathar[2] Christians of northern Italy and southern France that created the problem. The Cathars insisted on preaching the earlier doctrine of reincarnation. The Roman Church answered the challenge with the Inquisition.[3] The Church, using the flaming torch of this newly formed organization led by the Jesuits, killed hundreds of thousands of their fellow Christians under the pretext of saving the souls of those heretics who believed in that diabolical and dangerous doctrine. The Church leaders rightly realized that if they didn't eliminate the heresy of reincarnation they would lose their power over the people. The priesthood would lose its usefulness if such a heresy were allowed to flourish. The entire future of the Church was at stake.

It seems, then, dear readers, that historically the thinkers and leaders of the world, including those of Jesus' day — and indeed, Jesus himself — believed in the existence of the soul before birth; and that belief was deliberately downplayed and removed from the scriptures and other writings by both religious and state authorities.

Apart from that, does the idea of reincarnation have any *raison d'etre?* Does it make any sense for you? Would it help to explain anything in your life? Most of us have had unusual experiences that don't seem to have a normal or rational explanation. There have been times when we, upon meeting a stranger, are drawn inexplicably to him or her. We just *know* that we have met before, but as the song goes, we don't remember where or when. There have been times when we have felt great animosity toward an individual without any logical reason. Perhaps a certain city or country makes us nostalgic, even strangely homesick, or a particular historical epoch or event holds a strange fascination for us. Why? Is there any logical answer to explain these experiences, these feelings? Could it be that we are remembering the past — our very own past? Could it be that we may have lived on this earth before? Can the belief in reincarnation help to answer our questions about life, about death, about sin and judgment? I think it does. Let's consider the possibility a bit further.

In Revelation 13:9-10, the inspired St. John says, "If any man have an ear, let him hear. He that leadeth into captivity shall go into captivity: he that killeth with the sword must be killed with the sword. Here is the patience and the faith of the saints." Was he telling the truth? Do those who kill by the sword always die by the sword? Many murderers and other criminals die comfortably in their beds after lives of ease and pleasure. Where is the truth of sure retribution? Was John simply mistaken? Could he have understood wrongly? Had not Jesus used the same words in speaking to the disciples earlier?

Is there justice in life? Do you, my readers, believe that justice always prevails? Do you not see injustice all about you? Why is a person born blind, deaf, retarded, ugly or poor? Is it fair to be born without eyesight, to live your entire life without seeing a tree, a flower, a sunset or another human being, never knowing the warmth of a human smile? Is that justice from a loving God? Consider a retarded person. Is he condemned to a hell because he can't understand the rules of salvation? God is just, the scriptures claim. But is He just if one is born into a primitive society where he has never heard of Jesus or the Bible, or even had the chance to join the PTL Club? God is not just if that means that one must suffer everlasting hell because of his condition of birth. Or what about a youth born in a modern city who becomes a total wretch, dying in a stupor of drug overdose? Does he deserve eternal punishment? Is he not worth another chance? Is it justice to send him to a place of eternal punishment? I don't believe it is. I don't believe my friends reading this essay do either!

"Why me, O Lord?" How often have we expressed such a thought? "Why was I born with these limitations? With this sickly body? Why was I not born into a rich family, born with great talents? Why, why, why? It's not my fault that I was born lame, poor, ugly or without talent." Are we sure? Perhaps we *are* responsible! Let us examine these ideas from the viewpoint of cause and effect with the premise that *we are what we are because of what we were!* "What the entity is today is the result of what it has been in days and experiences and ages and aeons past. For life is continuous; and whether it is manifested in materiality or in other realms of consciousness, it is one and the same." These words of Edgar Cayce, spoken while in trance to a particular individual, express quite clearly the idea that our past does help to influence our present conditions.

Karma, the law of cause and effect, the law of compensation, is best expressed in the words of Jesus, "Whatsoever a man soweth, that shall he reap." Well, it seems, then, that our problems are our own doing. We ourselves are the cause of our difficulties and of our circumstances. Conversely, we who are healthy, beautiful, with many talents, successful and enjoying great blessings, are experiencing these things because we earned them! However, if we now take overly great pride in our beauty, riches or whatever and use our blessings unwisely, perhaps ridiculing those with less beauty, talent etc., we will pay in a future life, if not in this life.

The disciples of Jesus one day asked him, "Master, who did sin, this man, or his parents, that he was born blind?" Obviously if it were due to the man's sins, he must have sinned before he was born. ("If you have ears, hear.")

Gina Cerminara, in *Many Mansions,* perhaps the most influential book ever written on the subject of reincarnation, discusses many types of karma and gives a great number of illuminating examples based on the Edgar Cayce readings. An example of cause and effect resulting in a physical disability from the Cayce files is the story of a man who suffered from extreme digestive weakness. He was told by Cayce that he had in two successive lifetimes been a great glutton. Another example is that of a man who suffered anemia from birth. He had, five lifetimes previously, been a ruthless ruler in Peru where he had shed much blood.

An example of a karmic debt due to mockery concerned an 18-year-old girl, attractive but laughed at by her peers because of her being very overweight. In a previous lifetime in Rome as a beautiful and skillful athlete, she would ridicule the girls who were fat and had little athletic ability. A further example of the karma of mockery is that of a young Catholic man who in a previous life was a satirist in the French court and made much fun of homosexuals and what he considered their scandalous behavior. In this life his own homosexuality was making his life miserable due to the laughter and condemnation of others. Cayce concluded this particular reading with the words, "Condemn not then that you be not condemned. What you condemn in another, that you become in yourself."

It might appear to some of my readers that karma is something to be feared. But on the contrary, is it not a very reassuring concept to know that underlying all human affairs there is cosmic justice? If we know that our present life was not left to a capricious God, to nature or to chance but is the result of our own actions, we will not be left with a feeling of victimization, despair or disempowerment. We can have great hope and optimism for the future, knowing that as we handle our present problems and opportunities to the best of our ability, our life ahead will be a more beautiful and fruitful one. We can begin to feel the personal power that the collusion of church and state conspired to deny us.

Yes, God is a God of justice. Justice will be done. What a man sows he shall reap: If he kills, he will be killed. That is karmic law. That is justice. It is our karma to reap what we sow, but we have many lifetimes to learn, to live out our karma, to understand the consequences of our actions, to grow in the knowledge and wisdom of God. Lifetime after lifetime in this earthly vale of tears, we gradually tire of our lives of pain, sickness, degradation and loneliness. We finally get to the place where we say to ourselves, "There must be a better way." Then we begin the search in earnest, the search to find out who we are, the search for the God within, the search for the kingdom of heaven. When we begin the search, all the angels in heaven rejoice and cheer, standing ready to give us all the help we need (Luke 15:10).

All our pasts can be forgiven and forgotten. We can forgive ourselves for anything and everything we may have done in past lives. Completely understanding that we are and always have been a child of God, completely understanding and acknowledging that we never were separated from our Creator, we will give up all of our guilt. We will release our sense of unworthiness, our sense of sinfulness.

Our past is gone, forgiven, forgotten! We no longer will have to worry about any past karma catching up with us in this or in any future existence. We will no longer judge ourselves. We will rejoice, knowing that we are forever free. We are indeed God's son or daughter in whom He is well pleased. We will be ready to go on to higher realms of experience, to heaven, if you wish to call it that; and then no longer will we find it needful to return to this earthly vale of tears and be born once again into a physical body. We will be home – home with God.

---

[1]Rabbi Shneur Azlman, quoted in *Reincarnation, A New Horizon in Science, Religion, and Society* by Sylvia Cranston and Carey Williams. Julian Press, 225 Park Ave. S., New York, p. 193.

[2]The Cathars were the forerunners of the Waldensian Church of present-day Italy. Because of their long history they had been allowed to maintain some semblance of religious freedom during the period after the Lateran Pact of 1929 between Fascist Italy and the Vatican. That agreement between Mussolini and the papacy gave the Roman Church exclusive control over religious activity. Groups other than

the Waldensians, therefore, did not have the right to openly practice their religion until after the defeat of fascism, when, although intimidated and harassed by the priests and by the Christian Democratic government, they gradually became thriving religious communities once again. Only because of strong Communist Party influence was it possible. The Communists fought hard for religious freedom and often physically protected Protestants from harm.

For five months in Rome in 1947 I regularly attended a Baptist church and used to chuckle to myself when each Sunday morning the man who passed the offering plate had the Communist newspaper sticking out of his back pocket. Then I would read, with more amusement than amazement, the church newsletter in which a letter to the editor was signed, "A Group of Evangelical Communists." I wondered then how the folks back home in Minnesota would react if they knew that most Protestant Christians in Italy were Communists – at least when it came to marking their election ballots.

[3]Henry Charles Lea, *The Inquisition of the Middle Ages.* Macmillan Company, New York, 1961, pp. 41-112.

The God of the Old Testament

Thus shalt thou say unto the children of Israel, the Lord God of your fathers, the God of Abraham, the God of Isaac, and the God of Jacob . . .

— Exodus 3:15

The God of the Old Testament was *a man of war:* "The Lord is a man of war: The Lord is his name." (Exodus 15:3)

The God of the Old Testament was *a god of wrath:* ". . . thou sentest forth thy wrath, which consumed them [the enemy] as stubble." (Exodus 15:7)

The God of the Old Testament was *a jealous god:* ". . . for I, the Lord thy God am a jealous God." (Exodus 20:5)

The God of the Old Testament was *a god of fury:* ". . . for I will tread them in my anger and trample them in my fury." (Isaiah 63:3)

The God of the Old Testament was *a god of vengeance:* "To me belongeth vengeance and recompense." (Deuteronomy 32:35) "O Lord God, to whom vengeance belongeth." (Psalms 94:1)

The God of the Old Testament was *a god of retribution:* "And if any mischief follow, then thou shalt give life for life, eye for eye, tooth for tooth, hand for hand, foot for foot, burning for burning, wound for wound, stripe for stripe." (Exodus 21:23-25) "I will even appoint over you terror, consumption, and the burning ague, that shall consume the eyes and cause sorrow of heart: and ye shall sow your seed in vain, for your enemies shall eat it . . . I will punish you seven times more for your sins . . . and my soul shall abhor you." (Leviticus 26:16, 18, 30)

The God of the Old Testament *showed no mercy:* "And he that smiteth his father or mother, shall be surely put to death." (Exodus 21:15) "He that sacrifieceth unto any God, save unto the Lord only, he shall be utterly destroyed." (Exodus 22:20)

The God of the Old Testament *condoned slavery:* "And he said, cursed be Canaan; a servant of servants shall he be unto his brethren." (Genesis 9:25) ". . . for he [the slave] is his [master's] money." (Exodus 21:21)

The God of the Old Testament *condoned stealing:* "And they warred against the Midianites, as the Lord commanded Moses, and they slew all the males. . . . took all the women . . . and their little ones, and took the spoil of all their cattle, and all their flocks, and all their goods. And they burnt all their cities . . . " (Numbers 31:7, 9-10)

The God of the Old Testament *condoned murder and adultery:* "Now therefore kill every male among the little ones, and kill every woman that hath known man by lying with him. But all the women children that have not known a man by lying with him, keep alive for yourselves." (Numbers 31:17-18) "Thus saith the Lord, About midnight will I go out into the midst of Egypt: And all the firstborn in the land of Egypt will die . . . And there shall be a great cry throughout all the land of Egypt . . ." (Exodus 11:4-6)

The God of the Old Testament *rejoiced in the death of enemies:* "Then sang Moses and the children of Israel this song unto the Lord . . . I will sing unto the Lord, for he hath triumphed gloriously: the horse and his rider both hath he thrown into the sea." (Exodus 15:1)

The God of the Old Testament *showed racial prejudice, xenophobia and segregationist tendencies:* "And the Lord said unto Moses, Yet will I bring one plague more upon Pharaoh, and upon Egypt." (Exodus 11:1) ". . . that ye may know how the Lord God doth put a difference between the Egyptian and Israel." (Exodus 11:7) ". . . I will put none of these diseases upon thee, which I have brought upon the Egyptians: for I am the Lord that healeth thee." (Exodus 15:26) "Now therefore make confession unto the Lord God . . . and separate yourselves from the people of the land, and from the strange wives." (Ezra 10:11) "On that day they read in the book of Moses in the audience of the people . . . that the Ammonite and the Moabite should not come into the congregation of God for ever. . . . When they had heard the law that they separated from Israel all the mixed multitude." (Nehemiah 13:1,3)

The God of the Old Testament *demeaned women:* "But if her husband disallowed her . . . then he shall make her vow . . . of none effect . . ." (Numbers 30:8) "This is the law of jealousies, when a wife goeth aside to another instead of her husband, and is defiled: Or when the spirit of jealousy cometh upon him, and he be jealous over his wife, and shall set the woman before the Lord, and the priest shall execute upon her all this law. Then shall the man be guiltless from iniquity, and this woman shall bear her iniquity." (Numbers 5:29-31) "Behold now, I [Lot] have two daughters which have not known man; let me, I pray you, bring them out unto you, and do ye to them as you will: only unto these men do nothing." (Genesis 19:8)

The God of the Old Testament *saw ejaculate and menses as unclean:* "And if any man's seed of copulation go out from him, then he shall wash his flesh in water, and be unclean until the even. . . . And if a woman have an issue . . . she shall be put apart seven days: and whosoever toucheth her shall be unclean until the even." (Leviticus 15:16,19)

Enough! That doesn't sound like the God I love. I do not believe it sounds like the God that the readers know and love.

The God of the Old Testament was an anthropomorphic god. The God of the Old Testament exhibited the emotions, the weaknesses, the passions that mankind exhibits. Could a god of pure love have emotions, could he have weaknesses, could he show passion? If His love is all-encompassing, how could God exhibit and partake in all of the negativities of mankind?

The apocryphal book, "The Proclamation of Peter," a Gnostic text omitted from the canon by the early Church leaders, has passages that express utter horror that God, as described in the Old Testament, was actually believed by some to be our Father, our Creator God. The text questions that if the god so described really was our Creator, what hope could there be for humanity? Could we expect blessings and goodness from such a god? Could we seek mercy, compassion or forgiveness from such a god?

In *The Letters of Paul: A New Spiritual World View*, Paul says, "That God to which the Old Testament refers is not, beloved ones, is not the Supreme Godhead. The one whom the Old Testament Bible refers to as Jehovah is not the Supreme First Cause. . . . He was, rather, a racial god; one of the gods of this world."[1]

It seems to me that we should just accept the Old Testament at its word: that Jehovah was the god of Abraham, Isaac and Jacob and fought for the loyalty of the Israelite nation, contending against all other gods.

In the New Testament Jesus spoke out strongly against the precepts of the Old Testament God, proclaiming a new gospel, a gospel of love. In Matthew 5:38 he says, "Ye have heard that it hath been said, An eye for an eye and a tooth for a tooth: But I say unto you that ye resist not evil . . ." And again in verses 43-44 he says, "Ye have heard that it hath been said, Thou shalt love thy neighbor and hate thine enemy. But I say unto you, Love your enemies, bless them that curse you, do good to them that hate you, and pray for them which despitefully use you and persecute you."

That sounds like Jesus was speaking about his Father, the Supreme Godhead, the First Cause. He was speaking about my God! He was speaking about your God!

---

[1]Hilarion, *The Letters of Paul,* pp. 63, 172.

✧ 21

Judgment

Pass no judgment, and you will not be judged. For as you judge others, so you will yourselves be judged, and whatever measure you deal out to others will be dealt back to you. Why do you look at the speck of sawdust in your brother's eye with never a thought for the great plank in your own?

— Matthew 7:1-3

You are standing in the supermarket checkout line. Today, instead of reading the gossip in the tabloids to pass the time, you become a people-watcher. In your mind you begin to criticize each one you see: Why is she so fat? Couldn't she go on a diet? That man is so dirty, he should shave and put on some clean clothes — he's ugly enough as it is. Why is that old woman wasting my time haranguing the checkout lady? Why doesn't the bagger ask whether I want paper or plastic? Guess he's just dumb or lazy. Anyway, he's kind of weird-looking with that ridiculous haircut.

It's easy, isn't it, to judge and criticize everyone around us, from our wife or husband, our children, our boss, our subordi-

113

nates, the preacher, our neighbors and even the President of the United States? But could we not practice a little tolerance and practice accepting others as they are? When in line at the check-out counter we can look at each person with love even while we recognize their physical imperfections. We can look beyond the physical and remember that within each body there is a soul, a child of God. We can be aware that each person we come into contact with and even those we read about are doing the best they know how with the understanding they have.

Each of us is at a different point in our soul's development. The one we criticize may act negatively in things they little understand whereas others may know truths we have not yet experienced.

In Matthew 7 it says that if we do not judge others we will not be judged. We attract to ourselves the same energy that we send to others. If we accept our brother with understanding and compassion, we will receive the same understanding and compassion from him. First we must learn to forgive ourselves; then it will be easy to forgive others.

But how we love to judge others! Why do we not see the log in our eye before we criticize the small splinter in our brother's?

And we love to judge ourselves. How the Fundamentalist loves to beat his chest, proudly exulting that he is a sinner, often bragging that he is or was a bigger sinner than others. How the Christians flock to hear the visiting evangelist from another city who is billed as a former gangster! The worse his sin has been, the more the crowd wants to hear him. We love to call ourself a sinner and display our guilt. Loudly proclaiming our guilt somehow seems to lessen its pain.

As Emmanuel says in the following passage[1], if we learn to accept ourselves and others, there will be no need for forgiveness and no need to feel guilty.

> How can you not forgive yourself for being exactly who you are?
>
> To find the God within you you must go through the portal of self-acceptance as you are now.
>
> Yes, all your faults and imperfections, all your little secrets, fearful uglinesses that you are loathe to admit to yourself, are already known. They are part of the Divine Plan.
>
> True acceptance is saying, "It's all right, it's all right, it's all right."
>
> Self-acceptance bypasses the need for self-forgiveness.

The writer of Matthew 7 is not in any way saying that if we judge others, God will judge us. God does not judge. He sees us clearly for what we are – his sons and daughters, who are as pure, perfect and eternal as Himself. Jesus achieved Christhood when he became fully conscious that he was a son of God, and told his disciples that they were too ("You are one with me as I am one with the Father"), that God would not judge them and that they should not judge one another.

But because of their feelings of guilt they could not really accept the idea that they were truly sons of God, that they were one with Jesus. They insisted that they needed a savior, someone outside of themselves to save them from their sins. They believed that they could become the adopted sons of God, but never quite understood the message of Jesus that everyone was indeed a child of God.

When we can see ourselves as children of God, knowing that we – the real self, the Christ within – are perfect, sinless creatures, we cannot but accept ourselves and love ourselves without reservation. Then our love will embrace the whole world and the whole world will embrace us! Our entire being will shine with the love and joy of our Creator. Our love and joy will be apparent to everyone. No longer will we blame someone or something for anything in our lives, because if we do we realize that we are really blaming ourselves. Worse, we are blaming God.

It has been for me, and I believe for most of my readers, very difficult to accept the fact that we are all without sin and guiltless. When we look at ourselves, our actions, our thoughts, and when we look at the actions of those about us, we certainly feel that we must be guilty. We judge ourselves guilty. We judge those about us guilty. Yes, while we are living on this planet and clothed in our physical bodies we are forgetful of who we are and act through an ignorant ego, but in the eternity of God we are His perfect children. There is no sinful past, no future, but only the eternal present in God.

Why did the mob condemn Jesus to death? Was it not because he claimed that the son of God was guiltless? The mob in Jerusalem became furious, believing that Jesus' claim of innocence was blasphemy. We, in our egos, are still demanding crucifixion of ourselves, demanding that we pay the price for our guilt. All we need do is accept the truth of who we are and the atonement is ours. Should we not take God at His word? Let us not call God a liar. Let us not deny the words of Jesus. God's son is guiltless.

The Last Judgment! What a frightening prospect! We picture ourselves standing the "last day" before God, who sits on His throne with Jesus standing at His right side. God looks directly into our eyes and is about ready to make His last judgment of us. He will either say, "Depart from me into outer darkness. I never knew you. You are condemned to suffer everlasting punishment in a hell I have prepared for you," or He will pass us through the pearly gates into the kingdom of heaven where we will walk on streets paved with gold and be given a harp to play and sing His praises for eternity.

Is not the above a fair description of the average Christian's image of the Last Judgment? Let's examine some of the details of that picture. First, it is very anthropomorphic, is it not? We have a God in the form of a man (looks a lot like our paintings of Moses, doesn't He?) sitting on a throne with Jesus, who appears in his earthly, physical form at God's right side. Then we have the gates of pearl that lead into the kingdom of heaven — obviously a physical location of some magnitude where the streets are paved with gold. (We will still love our material riches, it seems.)

Where is heaven? Did not Jesus say in response to a disciple's question that the kingdom of heaven was in them — that *we* (our souls) are the kingdom of heaven?

And what about hell in our picture of the Last Judgment? If

heaven is up there somewhere, then hell must be down below somewhere. But God must be there, too, if He is present everywhere (He *is* omnipresent, is he not?). And is not God pure love? Could love prepare a hell with everlasting punishment of fire and brimstone and the "wailing and gnashing of teeth" (shades of Dante!)?

Obviously, the Last Judgment is badly misinterpreted and misunderstood by the average Christian. As described above, the Last Judgment has been and is yet utilized by hellfire-and-brimstone preachers to scare their followers into accepting their brand of religion. But nothing could be further from the truth.

Let's go back to that dramatic scene where we are standing before God awaiting His judgment. Is it even conceivable that our Creator would not recognize his Creation, His own son? Can God judge humanity, a creation of His, part of His own being? Is it conceivable that God could separate part of Himself from Himself? Is it not insanity to think so? Is it not arrogant to call God a liar, for He has proclaimed His son guiltless? Apparently we think we know better, and proclaim ourselves sinners and worthy of eternal punishment.

There never has been any judgment on the part of God. Only after the Separation, when we fled from the Garden of Eden, has there been the concept of judgment, the idea of choosing between what is good and what is evil. The only judging that has been done and is being done is by ourselves of ourselves. The "final judgment" of ourselves by ourselves will not entail any punishment; on the contrary, it will heal our sense of separation from God and release us from all of our guilt and pain.

It seems to me that judgment is a continuing process we go through during our lives on earth until we realize that we do not need to seek salvation through priests, rituals or adherence to any set of rules or dogmas, whether of a fundamentalist or other religious persuasion. The case that man has built against himself would have to be dismissed by the highest ultimate court because there can be no case against a son or daughter of God, for that is tantamount to a case against God.

The Last Judgment for each of us will be the moment when we know fully that God has already judged us perfect. It will happen when we finally realize that we do not need God's forgiveness and when we can accept ourself as a perfect, sinless creature. The Last Judgment for each of us will be when we finally hear the words of God welcoming us home — home with Him whom we never left! Jesus put it this way[2]:

> This is God's Final Judgment: "You are still My holy Son, forever innocent, forever loving and forever loved, as limitless as your Creator, and completely changeless and forever pure. Therefore awaken and return to Me. I am Your Father and you are My Son."

---

[1]*Emmanuel's Book,* p. 102.

[2]*A Course in Miracles, Workbook,* p. 445.

✧ 22

Forgiveness

Forgiveness . . . is still, and quietly does nothing. It offends no aspect of reality, nor seeks to twist it to appearances it likes. It merely looks, and waits, and judges not.

— from *A Course in Miracles*

It is easy to say, "I forgive you," but it is difficult for us to truly forgive. Often we say that we forgive someone without really meaning it. We say "I forgive you" to our child, to our spouse or to a friend. Perhaps it is after a mild family disagreement or after some more serious differences with a friend or co-worker. But do we always mean it when we say it? Do we sometimes inwardly say, "Yes, I forgive you this time, but I'll always remember what you did to me, and you'd better not do it again"? Is that truly forgiving?

If we truly forgive someone for what they did or said to or about us, we would really forget the incident, restoring our relationship with that person to what it was *before* the incident. True forgiveness (fore-giveness) implies that it never happened.

But why in the first place do we find it necessary to forgive? The need for forgiveness implies the perception that someone has attacked us. If we forgive someone for attacking us, it means that we have seen sin or wrongdoing in the attacker. We are saying to him, in effect, that even though he has done something terribly wrong, we will forgive him (and perhaps pray for his sinful soul). Are we not thus establishing the sin and then forgiving it? That is a contradiction.

When we forgive wrongdoing in others or when we acknowledge sin in our own life, we are identifying others and ourselves with the body. Only a body can be hurt. The real self, the soul, the divine part of us, cannot suffer.

Recall, from earlier essays, that we are not a physical body. Each of us is an eternal spirit of pure love, a part of the oneness of all. How, then, can we forgive a spirit of which we are part for doing wrong? The physical body is part of the illusion, part of our dream. As long as we believe in the body and in the existence of sin, we will find it necessary to forgive. When we realize that there is no sin — that is, when we realize that we were never separated from God — we will understand that there is no need either to forgive or to seek forgiveness. We never left God; we are still His son or daughter in whom He is well pleased.

The above notwithstanding, we are still experiencing this unreal world, and as long as we are in a physical body, we will exhibit the so-called sins of the flesh. We will lose patience, we will get angry, we will get frustrated, we will have periods of depression and we may commit "sins" of a much more serious nature. So as long as we are living in this world of time and space we need forgiveness as a means of restoring our awareness of God in our life.

Before we look at forgiveness and see how we can use it in healing the supposed separation from our Creator, let us examine how we usually deal with our sins and guilt in our daily life.

To begin with, our *belief* in sin is the source of all guilt. Sin ultimately is the belief or concept that we are separated from God. This belief created our ego. Our ego really is the belief in a separated self. The belief in separation created our physical world, including our world of human bodies.

Guilt arose from our belief in separation. We feel guilty for disobeying God, so we feel that we deserve punishment. We believe that we are opposing and attacking our Creator, so we accept as perfectly natural and reasonable the belief that God will oppose and attack us.

It seems that we cannot tolerate this overwhelming feeling of guilt, so we find ways of easing our pain and remorse. One way we suppress our feelings of guilt is through denial. We deny our guilt. Our ego tells us to pretend that our sin does not exist. We blot it out of our memory. We tell ourselves that it never happened. We put our sins out of mind and out of reach, but they are still there and will resurface when least wanted or expected.

If denial is not enough to make our guilt tolerable, we resort to projecting our guilt onto others. All of our troubles, all of our faults, all of our shortcomings, are caused by somebody or something external to us. By projecting the blame on someone else we feel free of guilt. It isn't our fault, so we can feel free again, free of our burden. We feel justified in being angry or regretful. "If only he had not done that to me" or "if only that event had not occurred, everything would be all right." We might even go so far as to say, "The devil made me do it" (anything to put the blame on somebody or something external to us).

Ultimately, however, all of our problems originate within ourselves. The first thing we need to do is realize that we alone are responsible for everything that impinges on our life. We might say that this is the first step in a process of forgiveness. We undo the projecting of blame onto others. We realize that we cannot blame our problem, our condition, our sin, on anybody or anything else. The external world is part of our dream. It is not real. We cannot protect our guilt onto anything external, since nothing "real" is happening. We need to realize that we are creating our own pain and suffering, that the source of all of our pain and suffering is within our own mind. The problem is that we have believed the ignorant lies of the ego, which constantly tells us that we are sinful creatures, that we are guilty of having separated from the Creator.

To overcome the lies of the ego we need the Holy Spirit's help. The Holy Spirit is the communication link between God the Father and ourselves, the "separated" sons and daughters. With the Holy Spirit's help we look at our sin and guilt and withdraw our belief in what the ego has been telling us. God knows that we have never sinned, and the Holy Spirit communicates that truth, that understanding, to us and so we are healed of the belief in separation.

God will do the rest. When we no longer see ourselves as sinners and as guilty, when we accept the Holy Spirit's truth which he communicates to us, then the last step in the process of forgiveness has already taken place. Our fear of God (the avenging, judging Father) is gone and we are healed of all of our past illusions. Thus we can, with full understanding, with full acceptance, with complete love, call God our Father and call ourselves His son or daughter.

At this point the reader is probably asking if the above means that we should not forgive others, that we should not say, "I forgive you." No, not at all. As long as we still believe even unconsciously in separation, then we should practice forgiveness of others and therefore, ultimately, forgiveness of ourselves.

God forgave us before we were born. He forgave all mankind before the beginning of this world. His forgiveness is simply the pure love that He is. In actuality, His forgiveness is not forgiveness. He cannot forgive us for what we have never done. He cannot forgive us for what we are not guilty of. He never condemned mankind, for He sees us for what we are, a part of His very essence. If man were guilty, God Himself would be guilty!

But as long as man is on this planet, as long as the soul inhabits this physical body and as long as we continue our earthly sojourn in time, we need to learn how to say, not only with our lips but with our heart, "I forgive you." In the process of forgiving others, gradually we will come to the understanding that we are at the same time forgiving ourselves. As long as we believe in separation, as long as we act in an I-Thou relationship, the act of forgiveness gradually teaches us that the one forgiven and the one forgiving are really part of the One. The belief of the ego in separation is undone by our joining with the Holy Spirit in true forgiveness.

I don't believe that God expects us to become saints overnight. But by asking the Holy Spirit for help, we can learn the art of true forgiveness. Our relationship with others is our practice field. The more difficult the relationship, the greater the opportunity for learning forgiveness. We should be thankful for our friends, for our fellow workers, for the boss or whoever it might be who creates the most difficult situations and problems in our life. It is through the process of forgiveness in such situations that our greatest learning takes place.

It is easier to forgive when we keep in mind that each person is at a different stage in his soul's development and that each person is doing the very best he knows how with his present understanding. We forgive the person though not condoning the deed he may have committed. A murderer must be separated from society, but we can completely forgive him, knowing that we are forgiving ourselves for the murderous thoughts we have had. We recognize in the murderer our true brother, for we are one. We must look upon our brother and see him as he truly is. Each one of us, as God's son or daughter, is perfect. We would not be His sons and daughters if we were not perfect. As Jesus says in *A Course in Miracles,* the only way to think of our brother is this: "I thank you, Father, for your perfect Son, and in his glory will I see my own."[1]

In this essay on forgiveness we have just scratched the surface. I highly recommend the book *Forgiveness and Jesus* by Kenneth Wapnick (see Reading List) for an exhaustive treatment of the subject.

126

To close this short essay I am adding this prayer by Jesus that many believe to be the actual words of the traditional Lord's Prayer.[2]

> Forgive us our illusions, Father, and help us to accept our true relationship with You, in which there are no illusions, and where none can ever enter. Our holiness is Yours. What can there be in us that needs forgiveness when Yours is perfect? The sleep of forgetfulness is only the unwillingness to remember Your forgiveness and Your Love. Let us not wander into temptation, for the temptation of the Son of God is not Your Will. And let us receive only what You have given, and accept but this into the minds which You created and which You love. Amen.

---

[1] *A Course in Miracles, Text,* p. 595.

[2] *Ibid.,* p. 326.

The Second Coming

I am with you alway, even unto the end of the world.
— Matthew 28:20

"The end of history as we have experienced it is just around the corner. The end of this age is fast approaching." These thoughts or beliefs are shared by many people throughout the world, Christians and non-Christians.

This is not about gloom and doom. The end of this age does not mean physical destruction of our planet or the elimination of human life upon it. The physical world will end only after we no longer need it for our experiencing. History will be no more when we realize that we are not of this world, when we realize that we are divine beings, citizens of the real world, at one with God.

Ever since Jesus' ascension two thousand years ago Christians have looked forward to his return to this earth. The Christian belief is that the man Jesus will return in the same physical body that he used while on earth. But does the Second Coming refer to the historical Jesus or to the Christ, the coming of the Cosmic Christ? When Jesus spoke of the Second Coming, the phrase he used in Aramaic, the language of his place and time, simply means the "coming of Christ." There is nothing in his words to imply a *second* coming. Indeed, as indicated above in Matthew, Jesus said that the Christ would always remain with us.

The first coming of Christ occurred at the time of creation, the coming of the Christ as the son of God. "In the beginning was the word, and the word was with God, and the word was God. . . . And the word was made flesh, and dwelt among us." The coming of Jesus as an embodiment of the full consciousness of the Christ occurred two thousand years ago. Jesus' earthly life was the period in which the conception of Christ was received into the collective human consciousness. During that long period of time known as the Fall and Separation, humanity had gradually forgotten its true identity as a son of God. Mankind forgot that it was a Christ.

Now, two millennia after the planting of the seed by Jesus, the Christ consciousness will burst into full bloom. This the "second coming" of Christ. It is not any rebirth or return of the historical man, Jesus. Jesus himself in *A Course in Miracles* says, "The Second Coming of Christ means nothing more than the end of the ego's rule and the healing of the mind."[1] Our minds and hearts will be healed when we remember that we always were, are now and ever will be, one with Christ. The Second Coming is when men and women everywhere will come to that realization. A well-known Christian author puts it this way, "The Second Coming will be the time when Christ will awaken dressed in the physical bodies of an incarnate human family."[2]

For each of us individually, the Second Coming occurs for us when we are "born again." To be born again doesn't mean to respond emotionally to the fervent pitch of a Jimmy Swaggart or a Billy Graham and "accept Jesus as your personal savior." It does mean that we must become as a little child, accepting his words with a simple faith. We must, in a sense, die to our old sense of self as a vile, sinful creature and, through a change of consciousness, become aware, as Jesus told us, that we never were separated from our Creator and that we are indeed God's son in whom He is well pleased. We must become as totally innocent as babes, that is, totally unaware of fear and evil, finding complete assurance and rest in God. That is the Second Coming for us as individuals.

The Second Coming for mankind as a whole will occur at the closing moment of this present age. Every eye will see Christ and every tongue confess that they are one with Christ and the Father. The world is fast preparing for that day. The Mayans called this day the return of the gods and pinpointed its occurrence in the fast-approaching year of 2011 (see "A.D. 2011").

---

[1]*A Course in Miracles, Text,* p. 58.

[2]Ken Carey, *Terra Christa.* Uni-Sun/Stillpoint, Kansas City, Missouri & Walpole, New Hampshire, 1985, p. 106.

♦ 24

A.D. 2011

A pregnant moment, a quarter century. Throughout the universe, all conscious beings watch.

— Ken Carey in *Vision*

The moment has almost arrived. The long-awaited pregnant moment is just about here — December 21, 2011, the exact date chiseled in stone so long ago. Hundreds of years ago the Mayans of the Yucatan peninsula of Mexico communicated this date on their now-famous calendar stone. This date has been revealed to many great seers of the past, and recent channeled messages confirm it. It is at the precise moment of the winter solstice of the year 2011, the moment of the year when the sun reaches its most southerly point and is ready for its return journey to the north.

Scientists have speculated that ever since the Big Bang, the moment of creation, the cosmos has been expanding ever outward in all directions. (Imagine yourself in the center of a continually inflating balloon.) Soon, they believe, the expansion will cease and, after a moment of complete rest, contraction will commence, thus beginning the second half of the outbreathing and inbreathing cycle of God. Leading-edge scientists believe that the Big Bang took place more than ten billion years ago in a closed universe (one that goes through a cycle of expansion and contraction). "The universe is close to being closed, and that's what everybody is excited about."[1] This statement was made at the annual meeting of 1700 astronomers of the American Astronomical Society in January 1993.

This moment of no-time. This moment of eternity. This moment pregnant with such potential. What does it portend? What does it promise?

To better picture this moment of no-time, imagine the movement of the pendulum of a grandfather clock. The pendulum swings in an arc back and forth, one-half a cycle being completed by the movement of the pendulum from the extreme upper left to the extreme upper right. Begin by imagining the pendulum at the extreme upper left (the Big Bang, creation). Then for ten billion years the pendulum has been moving to the right and will reach the apex of its upward swing at the winter solstice of the year 2011. When the pendulum reaches that point, there is a split second of rest before it begins its descent. This split second when the pendulum is neither moving up or down, this split second of stillness, is a moment of eternity when time stands still. It is a moment of no-time, when all laws of physics will be temporarily suspended, a moment "when the creator will slip inside creation."[2]

The Mayans and other ancients called this the moment of

the return of the gods. Christians call it the Second Coming of Christ (see "The Second Coming").

Astrologers too are predicting unparalleled changes in the next quarter century. They foresee great physical transformations: earthquakes, volcanic eruptions and tidal waves of unprecedented fury, as well as man-made violence —wars and acts of terrorism. More important, they speak of the transformation of the human spirit and breakthroughs in communication and other scientific technologies. With the rare and powerful conjunction of Uranus and Neptune in the earth sign of Capricorn beginning in 1993, some of these changes are already visible to many. With Uranus moving into the sign of Aquarius (signaling, I believe, the real beginning of the Age of Aquarius) in early 1995 and Pluto entering the sign of Sagittarius, promising the world a revolution of spirituality, these unparalleled changes spoken of above will become apparent to almost everyone.

It seems to me that this imminent moment is what mankind has been waiting for and working toward ever since his first appearance in physical form on planet earth. Scriptures of all religions proclaim the sacredness and extreme importance of this moment of eternity.

Those of us who are living have chosen to witness these last days of the outbreathing of God. We have chosen to live in these exciting, fast-moving, electrifying days. We have elected to be here to do our part in this spiritual transformation. We want to witness the tremendous challenges, the last great battles of the forces of darkness when the controllers of the world attempt to hold back the spiritual revolution. We are here to witness the separation of the wheat from the chaff, the separation of those who fear from those who love.

Before that moment arrives the haters of this world will either learn the way of love and acceptance of all or they will depart. There will be ample methods for their departure —wars, disease and earth changes.

We can consider the time from man's first appearance on earth to the year 2011 as a period of prehistory, a preparation for our real birth and the beginning of a millennium during which the body of Christ prepares for massive lift-off of the souls on earth at the close of the thousand years.

During these last years before that moment when "something incomprehensible"[3] (as a channeled message puts it) will occur, we should be making sure that we are living in love and not holding on to fear. Those who live in fear —who imagine the worst in people, who continue to blame others, who despise their fellows because of race, religion, sexual orientation or whatever, who claim that they are "saved" and others "lost" —are the haters, the ones living in fear. These are the chaff that shall be separated out. These will not take part in the transformation of A.D. 2011. But let's not worry too much about them, because they are not lost forever. They will continue their cycles of birth and death in a place where they can no longer affect those who embrace transformation until at some future time they choose love. As the scriptures proclaim, God is not willing that one soul be lost. And I think we can all agree that no power in the universe can overcome or supersede the will of God.

After that moment of the winter solstice of the year A.D. 2011 the earth will still be here. Mankind will still be inhabiting it. It does not mean the end of the physical world, planet earth. It does not mean the end of man's life on earth. It does mean, however, that life will be vastly different from what it has been prior to the great transformation. No one can say exactly how life will be, but we are told that it will be a time of love, not hate. Wars will be a thing of the past. It will be a time of cooperation instead of competition. Incredible advances will be made in every field of endeavor. The planet will be thoroughly cleansed of all pollution, the earth will give forth a fullness of its bounty, expanding human population to thirteen billion souls. These souls will be busy preparing the body of Christ for its unified journey to the stars and beyond at the close of the great millennium of peace and love.

---

[1]"Satellite discovery suggests universe might stop expanding." Jim Erickson in *Arizona Daily Star,* January 5, 1993, p. 1A.

[2]Ken Carey, *Starseed Transmissions.* Uni Sun, Kansas City, Missouri, 1982, p. 22.

[3]*Ibid.,* p. 17.

Today

I am what I am and that's all I am.
— Popeye

Perhaps Popeye said it best. Today we are what we are. What we are today is a result of all of our yesterdays — the yesterdays of past lives and, perhaps more important, the yesterdays of this present incarnation.

We chose the life we have and all our experiences. We chose to have the pains, the sorrows and the joys. In short, we chose all the experiences we have had because we knew that it was these very experiences we needed to heal our separation from God and bring us ever closer to that day when we become fully aware of who we are. The entire purpose of our life on earth is to bring us to that knowledge of being, where we know that there is only One.

We have suffered, endured and enjoyed many lives on earth. We have been born, we have suffered, we have died. Finally each of us comes to the realization that there must be a better way.

When that realization comes, the soul goes to work and seeks to restore itself on the path back to God —Whom it never actually left.

It seems to me that most of us have chosen a path of pain, suffering and degradation to bring us to God. The history of Christianity shows that we have followed that path with deliberation, for the Church has taught self-denial and self-punishment (judgment, guilt and continual expiation). We have been taught that poverty is virtuous. We have been taught to suppress and even deny the sexual nature of our bodies; medieval monks would spend hours, days, decades on their knees on the cold, rough stone floors of their drafty cells praying that their sexual impulses would pass. They wore hairshirts to ever remind them of their sinful bodies. The greater their suffering, the more God would love them and reward them in heaven. Although people no longer follow the extremes of medieval times, they still believe that pain and suffering advances them on the path. And it does, in a way, for when we suffer, when we experience great fear (there are no atheists in foxholes), we turn to God for help.

But is it necessary to suffer before turning to God? From the deepest part of my being I feel a resounding *no*. Can we not seek God through joy and happiness as well? Must we suffer before we become conscious of God and His will in our life? As Bartholomew says, "If you can find God through pain, there has to be a way to find God through joy."[1]

In *A Course in Miracles*, Jesus teaches that as long as we seek enlightenment we will not find it. Only when we realize that we already are enlightened will we be enlightened. Only the full realization that we don't have to work out our salvation will we stop looking for pain and suffering to bring the awareness of God to us. We don't have to put on hairshirts, we don't have to spend hours on our knees for God to listen to us. We don't have to hide away in silence to find our divinity. We don't need to go daily or weekly to listen to a priest or minister expound on scriptures he little understands. We don't have to *do* anything to become who we are; we *are* who we are and have always been. Today we are the perfect, eternal, sinless son or daughter of God we have always been.

We can today, right now, stop feeling guilty for our past, stop feeling guilty for all of our sins, for all our emotions, feelings and thoughts that keep us from accepting ourselves for what we really are.

Today we can begin by accepting ourselves and our brothers and sisters for what they are. We can show them compassion and understanding for all their humanness and love them as sons and daughters of God. Today we can change our attitude and decide to send each other light and love, and to our planet as well. We can realize that our Mother Earth is a living organism too, and send love and light to her.

Finally, today, as Meister Eckhart admonished so long ago, "Let God be God in you."[2]

---

[1]Bartholomew, *Reflections of an Elder Brother.* High Mesa Press, Taos, New Mexico, p. 24.

[2]Matthew Fox, *Meditations with Meister Eckhart.* Bear & Co., Santa Fe, New Mexico, p. 52. The full verse from which the excerpt was

taken reads:

> *The more you seek God,*
> *The less you will find God.*
> *If you do not seek God*
> *you will find God.*
> *God does not ask anything else of you*
> *except*
> *that you let yourself go*
> *and let God*
> *be God*
> *in you.*

A Fundamentalist Questions a New Ager

What does a New Ager do when confronted by someone who, perhaps in intimidating fashion, demands to know what he means by claiming to be a New Ager? What does he answer when someone asks, "Are you born again? Is Jesus your savior? Don't you realize that you are going to hell unless you get saved?"

I believe that there are a few basic concepts that a spokesman for the New Age can be prepared to explain. Admittedly, all New Agers don't agree on everything, but I believe that most seekers on a spiritual path will accept as within the mainstream of New Age thought the ideas expressed by the New Ager (NA) in the following imaginary conversation with a Fundamentalist (F).

F: Let us start with the most basic question. Do you believe in God? I often hear that you New Agers claim that you are God. How can we all be God?

NA: Yes, we certainly do believe in God, but we don't see God as a Moses-like figure sitting on a throne with Jesus sitting at His right hand. To begin with, let me say that New Agers don't put limits on God. Contrary to the Fundamentalist, who sees God as a superhuman being, the New Ager does not envision an anthropomorphic God. God is being. God is light and energy. God is everything that is perfect and eternal. To put the answer simply and to the point, God is. As God answered Abraham, "I am."

Yes, some New Agers make the statement that they are God. What they mean, I think, is that they are part of God. The Creator created them, so they are not God the Father, but an extension of the very essence of the Father and as such are as pure, perfect and eternal as God Himself. Instead of saying that one is God, it would be more appropriate to say that one is a son of God. I imagine that the typical Christian would still find fault with that statement and insist that mankind, instead of being sons of God, are sons of the devil.

F: Yes, I think that most Fundamentalists would certainly find fault with the idea that all men are sons of God. Were not Adam and Eve cast out of the Garden of Eden for their sin, and ever since that event all humans have been born in sin and must find atonement? Did not Jesus die on the cross for our sins? Is it not the blood of Jesus that washes our sins away and makes us acceptable in the sight of God?

NA: Wow! That's a lot of questions. Let's take one at a time. If we can clearly understand what did and what did not happen in the Garden of Eden – and by the way, I believe that the Garden of Eden was the entire planet – the answers to those questions will be more readily understood. As we have already mentioned, God created the human as a perfect being, a creature that is an extension of Himself, a veritable part of Him. How, then, could mankind become separated from God? Can God separate part of Himself from Himself? Yes, humans believed themselves to be separated from their Creator in the Garden, but that belief was a projection of their guilt for having turned their back on the face of God.

Then two thousand years ago Jesus was sent by God to this earth to remind us that we are God's children, that we are not, nor ever were, separated from God and that we never can be apart from Him. Jesus became the full embodiment of the Christ consciousness — Jesus, the Christ, or the Christ, Jesus. (You know, there are many Christians who have attended Sunday school and years of church services and still think that Christ is the last name of Jesus.) Jesus came to remind us that we all have the Christ and the kingdom of heaven within us and that we are all "one in Christ." He taught us that the sonship is one, that we all are one with each other, one with him as he is one with the Father. We could use this analogy: Every cell in our body is a microcosm of the entire body, yet does not think of itself as an individual in competition with the other cells of the body. The cells of the heart do not fight with the cells of the lungs or the liver. They all work together because they know that they are part of one organism. Indeed, even the planets and other heavenly bodies are just cells of the unified organism of the entire cosmos.

F: Hold it a minute! In Romans 3:23 it says, "For all have sinned and come short of the glory of God," and Romans 6:23 reads, "The wages of sin is death, but the gift of God is eternal life through Jesus, the Christ." Can you then say that man is not a sinner? If we are all sons of God and created perfect, why then do we not act like it? The world is obviously a place of pain and suffering, a place of much evil, of much sin. It's a world filled with sinners. I'm a sinner. Are you not a sinner? Isn't everybody?

NA: Yes, we are indeed all sinners if you mean by that we have done many things in our lives that are wrong and perhaps evil. That is, evil and wrong in the eyes of man, evil and wrong as judged by society, judged by you and me. But if one defines sin as something that separates us from God, then we are not sinners and sin does not exist. God does not judge us. He sees us, His creation, for what it is – an extension of His very being and as pure and eternal as He is. Nothing can separate us from God because we are part of Him, as we explained earlier. In our physical self we certainly do commit all sorts of wrongs. As you say, even the very best of humanity is far from good. But the Christ within, what we *really* are, is perfect and is one with all mankind, one with Christ, one with God. In *A Course in Miracles,* Jesus made it very clear when he said, "You have never sinned but have been badly mistaken."

I'm glad you quoted Romans 6:23. That is one of my favorite verses, for it so clearly shows what I have been trying to say. Yes, man in his physical body certainly is not a perfect being. While we are in the body and follow the will of the ego we miss the mark of the high calling and fail miserably, and so our body will die. Humans "sin" and die. But the real you, the real me, the soul within the body, as ordained from the very beginning, is immortal. It can never die. If it could, God would not be God.

Yes, I truly believe that man is "lost." Yes, we have lost our way. Yes, we have lost our understanding. Yes, we have lost the remembrance of who we are. But, glory to God (I can't resist sounding like a fundamentalist preacher), we are not lost and going to any place of everlasting torment. The most "evil" person on earth is not lost in the sense of God denying him or sending him to hell. Eventually, each and every soul will find the path once again and choose love instead of fear. Do not the scriptures say that God is not willing that one soul be lost? What God wills *is!*

F: Well, your responses to my questions just might persuade me to rethink some of my ideas. But about my previous question, if what you say is true, why did Jesus die on the cross if it was not to save us from our sin? Or perhaps you New Agers don't believe that Jesus was crucified and ascended from the tomb?

NA: There is much recent scholarship questioning whether Jesus actually did die on the cross, but I personally believe that Jesus did go to the cross. I believe he died and rose again, and I think that most New Agers believe that. Christ did not die, however. It was Jesus, the son of man, who died. Christ, the son of God, did not die. Christ has existed from the beginning with God and exists today in every soul.

The body can be destroyed, but what is real, what is eternal, cannot be destroyed. The crucifixion once and for all taught us that. It was the supreme example for us that our bodies can be persecuted, tortured and even killed, but we, the sons of God, cannot be destroyed or assaulted in any manner. Jesus understood and believed that fully. That is why he did not consider that he was being assaulted or persecuted. The resurrection after the crucifixion releases us from all fear, for it showed that nothing can harm the son of God.

I would like to quote for you the words of Jesus in *A Course in Miracles,*

> Your resurrection is your reawakening. I am the model for rebirth, but rebirth itself is merely the dawning on your mind of what is already in it. God placed it there Himself, and so it is true forever. . . . The message of the crucifixion is perfectly clear: "Teach only love, for that is what you are."

F: Your responses to my questions so far seem to be logical and make a lot of sense to me, but before changing my cherished and long-held beliefs and concepts, I will have to carefully consider your arguments. If your arguments are correct, at least some of what you would call our Christian dogmas will have to be reconsidered. But now a different kind of question: Some televangelists and others condemn New Agers as satanists or members of weird cults of one kind or another. What do you have to say about that?

NA: We New Agers are well aware of the lunatic fringe of Fundamentalism attempting to discredit New Age teaching by lumping us together with the far-out cult groups — satanic worshippers etc. New Agers have nothing to do with such groups and avoid them as much as do the Fundamentalists. But we do not fear them nor do we hate them. On the contrary, we extend our love to those individuals who indulge in cultist practices, even to those who worship the devil. They too are sons and daughters of God. They too will sooner or later find their way back to a remembrance of that fact.

In speaking of cults, there is one thing I would like to say. Many Christians (and others, too) confuse the word "cult" with the word "occult." Occult simply means something for those "in the know," for the initiated, something secret or esoteric. As you may know, the Bible is the greatest occult book ever written, so it always amazes and amuses me when Fundamentalists condemn the occult. When Christianity began in the days of the Roman Empire, it was considered the most dangerous cult within the Empire. When it became the dominant religion it was no longer called a cult. For most people, a cult is any group, usually a small group, that they do not like.

F: So far everything we have discussed has been about religious or spiritual concepts and differences between the Fundamentalist's understanding and a New Age understanding. Is there anything else, any other ideas or beliefs that would generally characterize a New Ager?

NA: Yes, I think there are some commonly held attitudes and beliefs of most New Agers. Of course, many Fundamentalists and others would also find themselves holding the same beliefs and attitudes, but it is much more common among the New Age group. To begin with, since New Agers accept themselves and others just the way they are, recognizing that all souls are at different places on their path back to God and doing the best they can with the understanding they have at the time, they are in the forefront in working for civil rights for all. They believe in complete equality for the races, for women, for homosexuals and for any other group that may experience discrimination in any way. Likewise, New Agers are working for peace – peace between nations and peace between individuals and groups everywhere.

In health matters, New Agers often prefer holistic or natural healing methods to those that are drug-oriented, which are politcally entrenched at the moment. And of course, New Agers believe that humanity is properly the caretaker, not the exploiter or sub-jugator, of the world and its resources, and so they are involved in environmental groups working to clean up pollution in all of its aspects. In short, New Agers generally are very sympathetic, caring and nurturing individuals and feel that it is their responsibility to help whenever and wherever it is possible to do so.

F: Well, thank you for this interview today. This has been a very challenging experience for me and (dare I say it?) maybe even an enlightening one. I hope that those who will read the words of our discussion here today will find it challenging and enlightening also.

Reading List

A Course in Miracles. Foundation for Inner Peace, Huntington Station, New York, 1975. This is not a book to sit down and read through. It requires a patient, methodical and thoughtful study over a period of a year or more. The *Course* includes a Text, a Workbook for Students (one mental exercise a day for 365 days) and a Manual for Teachers. It was channeled by Jesus through Helen Shucman, a Jewish psychiatrist at Presbyterian Hospital in New York City.

Bartholomew, *From the Heart of a Gentle Brother.* High Mesa Press, Taos, New Mexico, 1987. This volume has additional essays of the same enlightening quality of the earlier book (below). It adds a question-and-answer section.

Bartholomew, *I Come as a Brother.* High Mesa Press, Taos, New Mexico, 1986. This book is to me one of the most beautiful and inspiring books ever written. It is channeled through Mary-Margaret Moore, who lives in New Mexico. The oneness of all is the central theme throughout its many essays.

Carey, Ken, *Starseed: The Third Millenium.* Harper San Francisco,

New York, 1991. These three channeled volumes are among the most inspiring, enlightening and reassuring books available. To be read again and again. In speaking about the source of the channeled information, Mr. Carey writes in the introduction to the first volume, "But by whatever term we choose to understand these entities, their purpose in sending these messages has not been to teach us of themselves, but to teach us of our own nature and purpose upon this third planet from the star we call Sun."

_____, *Starseed Transmissions*. Uni Sun, Kansas City, 1983.

_____, *Terra Christa*. Uni-Sun, Kansas City, 1985. This volume (not channeled) is highly recommended for all Bible students. Mr. Carey says in the introduction, "This book is about Christ. It tells an abridged tale of humanity's experience with its Creator. It is for anyone who still entertains the prospect of a New Heaven or New Earth. It is a book for Christians, for Jews, for mainstream churchgoers and agnostics alike. It is not recommended for anyone with arthritic understanding, unable to creak into new perspectives. It is a book about life, change, growth, healing, transformation and renewal. It is a book for my friends."

_____, *Vision*. Uni-Sun, Kansas City, 1985.

Cerminara, Gina, *Many Mansions*. Signet, New York, 1950. Perhaps the most influential book ever written on the subject of reincarnation. Ms. Cerminara's analysis is largely based on the Edgar

Cayce readings. A very thorough but highly readable volume.

Cranston, S. and C. Williams, eds., *Reincarnation: A New Horizon in Science, Religion and Society*. Julian, New York, 1984. The dust jacket for this large volume reads in part that this book "is the most comprehensive and effectively practical book ever published on the subject. Bringing together the work of internationally reputable scientists, social historians, and prominent psychologists, it presents the reader with the best that has been thought and written on this important area of human life."

Essene, Virginia, *New Teachings for an Awakening Humanity*. S.E.E. Publishing Co., Santa Clara, California, 1986. Channeled by the Christ consciousness through Virginia Essene, this highly important book explains clearly God's purpose in creation and our role as sons and daughters of God. Emphasized the necessity of peace and of better stewardship to save our planet.

Fogg, Bob and Ron Goettsche, *Down to Earth*. Synergy, Denver, 1984. Inspiring and enlightening essays on many subjects, including love, death, creation, relationships. I have quoted from the essay on sexuality in this book.

Fox, Matthew, *The Coming of the Cosmic Christ*. Harper & Row, New York, 1988. In a more recent work, the author, a Roman Catholic priest, presents a paradigm shift for Christianity and for the world at large from the "quest for the historical Jesus" to the "quest for the Cosmic Christ."

_____, *Meditations with Meister Eckhart*. Bear & Co., Santa Fe, New Mexico, 1983. A thrilling small volume of the writing of a medieval mystic who was declared a heretic. He wrote bravely of the divinity of man and the oneness of man with his Creator.

_____, *Original Blessing*. Harper & Row, Inc., New York, 1983. The author shows clearly and convincingly from the scriptures that man was not born with original sin (sin does not exist), but with original blessing as a child of God, a creation of God —indeed, a part of God.

Friedman, Norman, *Bridging Science and Spirit*. Living Lake Books, St. Louis, Missouri, 1994. In my opinion, this is absolutely essential reading for anyone who is really interested in understanding creation and reality from both a scientific and a spiritual viewpoint. The reader will learn that the two viewpoints differ only in terminology.

Hawking, Stephen W., *A Brief History of Time*. Bantam, New York, 1988.

Head, J. and S.L. Cranston, *Reincarnation in World Thought*. Julian Press, New York, 1967. An anthology of thought on the subject of reincarnation from earliest times to the present. Over 400 pages of fascinating quotations.

_____, *Reincarnation: The Phoenix Fire Mystery*. Julian Press,

New York, 1967. "An East-West dialogue on death and rebirth from the worlds of religion, science, psychology, philosophy, art, and literature, and from great thinkers of the past and present" (from the title page).

Hilarion, *The Letters of Paul.* Triad, Ashland, Oregon, 1989. Must reading for serious biblical students. The latest translations of the letters of Paul, with new insights into the original meaning of his writings.

Jampolsky, Gerald G., *Love is Letting Go of Fear.* Celestial Arts, Berkeley, California, 1988. A book of lessons, beautifully illustrated, in learning to love by letting go of fear. Based on *A Course in Miracles.*

_____, *Out of Darkness into the Light.* Bantam, New York, 1990. Dr. Jampolsky's story of the great influence *A Course in Miracles* had on his life.

Lea, Henry Charles, *The Inquisition of the Middle Ages.* Macmillan, New York, 1961.

Marciniak, Barbara, *Bringers of the Dawn.* Bear & Co., Santa Fe, New Mexico, 1992. We are members of the Family of Light, bringers of the dawn, remembering our beginnings and now creating a new reality on this planet. Channeled from the Pleiadians. I believe this to be one of the most important books of the early nineties. Must reading.

Mitchell, Steven, *The Gospel According to Jesus*. Harper Collins, New York, 1991.

Pagels, Elaine, *The Gnostic Gospels*. Random House, New York, 1979.

Puryear, Herbert Bruce, *Why Jesus Taught Reincarnation*. New Paradigm Press, Scottsdale, Arizona, 1992. Written by a Christian for Christians. Wonderful new insights into the truths of the Bible. Questions about the meaning of your life, your origin and your destiny are answered.

Roberts, Jane, *The Nature of Personal Reality*. Prentice Hall, Englewood Cliffs, New Jersey, 1974. Two of the many volumes channeled from the discarnate personality of Seth. Tremendous insights about the true reality of God, mankind and nature. More and more these insights are being arrived at separately by scientists working in the field of quantum physics.

_____, *Seth Speaks: The Eternal Validity of the Soul*. Prentice Hall, Englewood Cliffs, New Jersey, 1972.

Rodegast, Pat and Judith Stanton, compilers, *Emmanuel's Book*. Bantam, New York, 1985. Ram Dass in his introduction says, "Being with Emmanuel one comes to appreciate the vast evolutionary context in which our lives are being lived . . . And at each moment we are at just the right place in the journey." Highly inspirational and thought-provoking reading.

_____, *Emmanuel's Book II: The Choice for Love*. Bantam, New York, 1988.

Ryerson, Kevin and Stephanie Harolde, *Spirit Communication: The Soul's Path*. Bantam, New York, 1989. Various spirit entities channeled by Kevin Ryerson. Many subjects are dealt with. Inspiring messages of hope and transformation. Highly recommended.

Spong, John Shelby, *Rescuing the Bible from Fundamentalism*. Harper San Francisco, 1991. The author, a bishop of the Anglican Church, teaches a more liberal social view, as revealed in the Bible, than fundamentalist teachings. Must reading for those who want to better understand the teachings of the Bible.

Talbot, Michael, *The Holographic Universe*. Harper Collins, New York, 1991. The latest science written for the layman. The concept of the universe as one great hologram helps to answer the question, "What is reality?"

Wapnick, Kenneth, *Forgiveness and Jesus*. Foundation for "A Course in Miracles," Roscoe, New York, 1990.